OECD Development Co-operation Peer Reviews: Iceland 2017

This work is published under the responsibility of the Secretary-General of the OECD. The opinions expressed and arguments employed herein do not necessarily reflect the official views of OECD member countries.

This document and any map included herein are without prejudice to the status of or sovereignty over any territory, to the delimitation of international frontiers and boundaries and to the name of any territory, city or area.

Please cite this publication as:
OECD (2017), *OECD Development Co-operation Peer Reviews: Iceland 2017*, OECD Publishing, Paris.
http://dx.doi.org/10.1787/9789264274334-en

ISBN 978-92-64-27432-7 (print)
ISBN 978-92-64-27433-4 (PDF)

Series: OECD Development Co-operation Peer Reviews
ISSN 2309-7124 (print)
ISSN 2309-7132 (online)

The statistical data for Israel are supplied by and under the responsibility of the relevant Israeli authorities. The use of such data by the OECD is without prejudice to the status of the Golan Heights, East Jerusalem and Israeli settlements in the West Bank under the terms of international law.

Corrigenda to OECD publications may be found on line at: *www.oecd.org/about/publishing/corrigenda.htm*.
© OECD 2017

You can copy, download or print OECD content for your own use, and you can include excerpts from OECD publications, databases and multimedia products in your own documents, presentations, blogs, websites and teaching materials, provided that suitable acknowledgement of OECD as source and copyright owner is given. All requests for public or commercial use and translation rights should be submitted to *rights@oecd.org*. Requests for permission to photocopy portions of this material for public or commercial use shall be addressed directly to the Copyright Clearance Center (CCC) at *info@copyright.com* or the Centre français d'exploitation du droit de copie (CFC) at *contact@cfcopies.com*.

Conducting the peer review

The OECD Development Assistance Committee (DAC) conducts periodic reviews of the individual development co-operation efforts of DAC members. The policies and programmes of each member are critically examined approximately once every five years, with six members examined annually. The OECD Development Co-operation Directorate provides analytical support, and develops and maintains, in close consultation with the Committee, the methodology and analytical framework – known as the Reference Guide – within which the peer reviews are undertaken.

The objectives of DAC peer reviews are to improve the quality and effectiveness of development co-operation policies and systems, and to promote good development partnerships for better impact on poverty reduction and sustainable development in developing countries. DAC peer reviews assess the performance of a given member, not just that of its development co-operation agency, and examine both policy and implementation. They take an integrated, system-wide perspective on the development co-operation and humanitarian assistance activities of the member under review.

The peer review is prepared by a team, consisting of representatives of the OECD Development Co-operation Directorate working with officials from two DAC members who are designated as "examiners". The country under review provides a memorandum setting out the main developments in its policies and programmes. Then the review team visits the capital to interview officials, parliamentarians, as well as civil society and non-governmental organisations representatives of the donor country to obtain a first-hand insight into current issues surrounding the development co-operation efforts of the member concerned. The field perspective is gained by assessing how members are implementing the major DAC policies, principles and concerns, and reviewing practices in recipient countries, particularly with regard to poverty reduction, sustainability, gender equality and other aspects of participatory development, and local aid co-ordination. The peer review team consults representatives of the partner country's administration, parliamentarians, civil society and other development partners.

The Secretariat then prepares a draft report on the member's development co-operation which is the basis for the DAC review meeting at the OECD. At this meeting senior officials from the member under review respond to questions formulated by the Committee in association with the examiners.

This review contains the main findings and recommendations of the Development Assistance Committee and the analytical report of the Secretariat. It was prepared with examiners from Greece and Slovenia for the peer review of Iceland on 8 March 2017.

Table of contents

Conducting the peer review 3

Abbreviations and acronyms 7

Iceland's aid at a glance 9

Context of the peer review of Iceland 11

The DAC's main findings and recommendations 13

Secretariat's report..23

Chapter 1: Towards a comprehensive Icelandic development effort 25

    Global development issues 25
    Policy coherence for development 26
    Financing for development 28

Chapter 2: Iceland's vision and policies for development co-operation 31

    Policies, strategies and commitments...31
    Approach to allocating bilateral and multilateral aid..32
    Policy focus 34

Chapter 3: Allocating Iceland's official development assistance 39

    Overall ODA volume 39
    Bilateral ODA allocations 41
    Multilateral ODA channel 43

Chapter 4: Managing Iceland's development co-operation 47

    Institutional system 47
    Adaptation to change 50
    Human resources 51

Chapter 5: Iceland's development co-operation delivery and partnerships 55

    Budgeting and programming processes..55
    Partnerships 58
    Fragile states 61

Chapter 6: Results management and accountability of Iceland's development co-operation.....65

    Results-based management system..65
    Evaluation system...66
    Institutional learning 68
    Communication, accountability and development awareness 69

Chapter 7: Iceland's humanitarian assistance..75

    Strategic framework 75
    Effective programme design 76
    Effective delivery, partnerships and instruments 77
    Organisation fit for purpose 79
    Results, learning and accountability...80

Table of contents

Annex A: OECD/DAC standard suite of tables 83
Annex B: Organisational structure 91
Annex C: Perspectives from Malawi, Mozambique, Uganda on Icelandic development co-operation 93

Tables

Table 4.1 Number of staff (full-time equivalent), 2012-16 51
Table 5.1 Iceland's progress against selected aid effectiveness targets, 2009-2015 57
Table A.1 Total financial flows 83
Table A.2 ODA by main categories 84
Table A.3 Bilateral ODA allocable by region and income group 85
Table A.4 Main recipients of bilateral ODA 86
Table A.5 Bilateral ODA by major purposes 87
Table A.6 Comparative aid performance 88
Table A.7 Comparative aid performance to LDCs 89

Figures

Figure 3.1 Trends in Iceland's net ODA, 1999-2015 40
Figure 3.2 Share of Iceland's gross bilateral ODA allocable by region, 2014-15 42
Figure 3.3 Iceland's official development assistance to multilateral organisations, 2011-15 44
Figure 4.1 Iceland's new development co-operation system 49
Figure A.1 Net ODA from DAC countries in 2015 90
Figure B.1 Organigram of the Ministry for Foreign Affairs 91
Figure B.2. Iceland's Team on International Development Co-operation 92
Figure C.1 Icelandic ODA disbursements to Malawi, Mozambique and Uganda 2011-14 94

Boxes

Box 1.1. Iceland's advocacy for gender 26
Box 2.1 Iceland's support for the United Nations University in Reykjavik 34
Box 5.1 Example of Iceland's scenario planning 56
Box 5.2 The regional geothermal energy programme in East Africa draws on Iceland's expertise and builds partnerships for leverage and scale up 59
Box 6.1 Iceland's new communications strategy 71

Abbreviations and acronyms

CCOE	NATO Civil-Military Cooperation Centre of Excellence
CERF	Central Emergency Response Fund
COHAFA	Working Party on Humanitarian Aid and Food Aid
CRS	Creditor Reporting System
CSR	Corporate Social Responsibility
CSSPS	Civil Society Platform for Peacebuilding and Statebuilding
DAC	Development Assistance Committee
DDC	Department of Development Cooperation
EADRCC	Euro-Atlantic Disaster Response Coordination Centre
EaP	Eastern Partnership
EED	European Endowment for Democracy
EU	European Union
FDI	Foreign direct investment
FIU	Financial Intelligence Unit
GENE	Global Education Network in Europe
GHD	Good Humanitarian Donorship
GIZ	Deutsche Gesellschaft für Internationale Zusammenarbeit
GNI	Gross national income
HIPC	Heavily indebted poor country
ICRC	International Committee of the Red Cross
IDA	International Development Association
IDPs	Internally displaced persons
INCAF	International Network on Conflict and Fragility
ISAF	International Security Assistance Force
LDCs	Least developed countries
MFA	Ministry of Foreign Affairs
NGO	Non-government organisation
NOHA	Network on Humanitarian Action
OCHA	Office for the Coordination of Humanitarian Affairs
ODA	Official development assistance
OECD	Organisation for Economic Co-operation and Development
OOF	Other official flows
OSCE	Organization for Security and Co-operation in Europe

Abbreviations and acronyms

PCD	Policy coherence for development
PISA	Programme for International Student Assessment
SDGs	Sustainable Development Goals
SRD	Strategy for Responsible Development
UN	United Nations
UNDO	United Nations Development Organization
UNDP	United Nations Development Programme
UNRWA	United Nations Relief and Works Agency for Palestine Refugees in the Near East

Signs used:

ISK	Icelandic Króna
EUR	Euro
USD	United States dollars
( )	Secretariat estimate in whole or part
-	(Nil)
0.0	Negligible
..	Not available
...	Not available separately, but included in total
n.a.	Not applicable
p	Provisional

Slight discrepancies in totals are due to rounding.

Annual average exchange rate: 1 USD = ISK

2010	2011	2012	2013	2014	2015
122.2420	116.0580	125.1180	122.1541	116.6880	131.8961

Iceland's aid at a glance

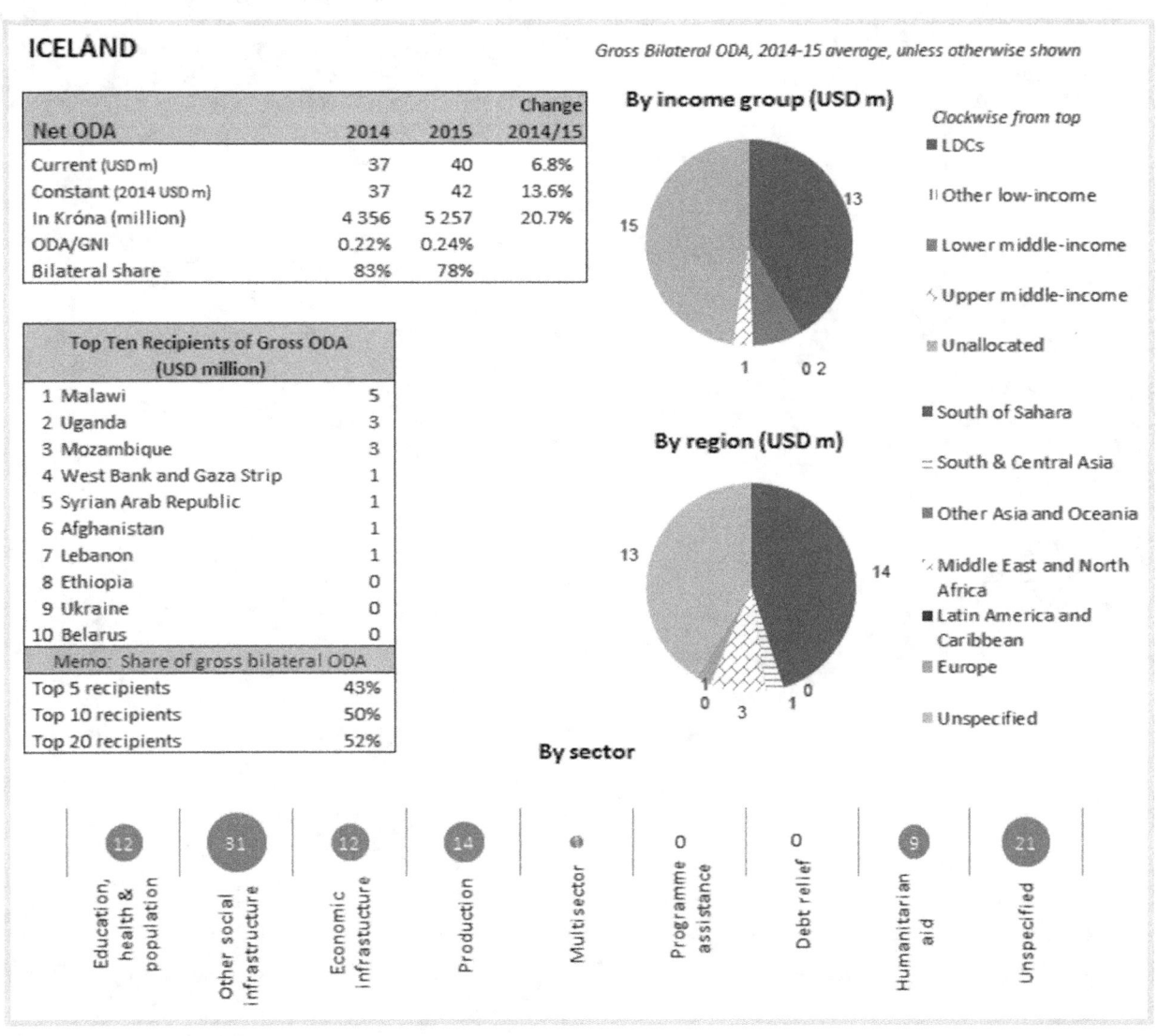

Source: OECD-DAC; www.oecd.org/dac/stats/aid-at-a-glance.htm

Context of the peer review of Iceland

With just 330 000 people dotted over a land mass of 103 000 square kilometres, Iceland is the most sparsely populated country in Europe. In addition to having one of the highest life satisfaction ratings of all OECD countries, Iceland also boasts the highest employment rate. While Iceland still has a lower gross national income per capita than other Nordic countries (USD 46 606), wage growth is in double digits and the income inequality gap is the narrowest of all OECD countries.

Iceland's economy is driven by the aluminium and fisheries industries and – increasingly – by tourism. Agriculture remains a key source of employment, accounting for 7% of gross domestic product, with dairy and sheep meat being the most important products. Following the 2008-2011 financial and banking crisis, the economy is now booming, with an expected growth rate of around 5% in 2016, which is faster than any other OECD country. Inflation is low, at around 2% in 2016, and has been held down by exchange rate appreciation. The economy has also been helped by falling energy prices: about 85% of Iceland's total primary energy supply is derived domestically from renewable sources, making Iceland the world's largest "green" energy and electricity producer per capita. However, underlying inflationary pressures are high and monetary policy remains tight, which may slow growth in 2017. Key risks in the long term include overheating of the economy, low productivity, and high debt.

Key foreign policy priorities include environmental sustainability – clean oceans, renewable energy and the fight against climate change – gender equality, trade liberalisation and development co-operation. Moreover, respect for human rights and the peaceful resolution of disputes are defined as cornerstones of Iceland's foreign policy, which is anchored in a long experience as one of the world's oldest assembly democracies, with the country's first parliament (the Althingi) established in AD 930.

In recent years, mass anti-government protests sparked by the economic crisis made international headlines. In April 2016, following the release of the Panama Papers and further public protests, Iceland's Prime Minister stepped down. National elections held six months later – on 29 October 2016 – did not return a clear majority. As a result, Iceland's President requested the previous government to manage daily business in a caretaker capacity until negotiations for a new government were concluded. On 10 January 2017, a new conservative coalition government was agreed – comprising the Independence Party, Reform Party and Bright Future – with a majority of one seat.

Iceland's official development assistance (ODA) fluctuated wildly in the wake of the financial and banking crisis, reaching a peak of 0.36% of gross national income (GNI) in 2008 before descending to an average of 0.22% over the past five years. On current forward estimates, Iceland's ODA is scheduled to reach 0.26% of its GNI by 2018. Recent public opinion surveys show high levels of support for development co-operation but little understanding of it.

Sources:

ICEIDA (2013), *Survey of Public Attitudes on Development,* www.iceida.is/media/pdf/1307_Throunarsamvinna_final.pdf.
OECD (2016a), Population (indicator), http://dx.doi.org/10.1787/d434f82b-en, accessed 7 December 2016.
OECD (2016b), Gross domestic product (GDP) (indicator), http://dx.doi.org/10.1787/dc2f7aec-en, accessed 7 December 2016.
OECD (2016c), "How's life in Iceland?", OECD Better Life Initiative, OECD, Paris, May 2016, www.oecd.org/iceland/Better-Life-Initiative-country-note-Iceland.pdf.
OECD (2015a), *OECD Economic Surveys: Iceland 2015*, OECD Publishing, http://dx.doi.org/10.1787/eco_surveys-isl-2015-en
OECD (2014), *OECD Environmental Performance Reviews: Iceland 2014*, OECD Publishing, http://dx.doi.org/10.1787/9789264214200-en.

The DAC's main findings and recommendations

1 Towards a comprehensive Icelandic development effort

Indicator: The member has a broad, strategic approach to development and financing for development beyond aid. This is reflected in overall policies, co-ordination within its government system, and operations

Main findings

Iceland reached an important milestone as a provider of development co-operation when it joined the Development Assistance Committee (DAC) in 2013. Since then, Iceland has strengthened its strategic framework and systems for development co-operation by improving the alignment between development, foreign and trade policy and by expanding its diplomatic efforts on global development issues. The findings and recommendations of this first peer review provide a baseline to document Iceland's development co-operation activities and to help it progress over the medium term.

Iceland is a committed and active member of the international community, using its diplomatic influence in a strategic and effective way to address key international risks and shape global development in areas where it can add value: gender equality, geothermal energy, fisheries' management and land restoration. Despite its small diplomatic capacity and, more generally, small public administration, Iceland is successful at drawing on its own domestic experience, as well as on its long experience in development co-operation, to shape its foreign policy and engage upfront in international processes. In doing so, it has also enlisted the support of its national leaders, who leverage their political capital and partnerships for global development.

Iceland's successful efforts internationally on gender and equality, renewable energy, land restoration and oceans show how it rallies a range of actors behind a common objective. In particular, Iceland was engaged in international negotiations leading up to the 2030 Agenda for Sustainable Development in 2015 on all these issues, effectively advocating for a separate goal on each, and for gender to be mainstreamed across the goals. Iceland also championed the "HeforShe" campaign and organised a number of "Barbershop" conferences in 2015, aiming at rallying men and boys to uphold gender equality. These examples illustrate how Iceland is able to introduce cutting-edge perspectives into the global arena in its advocacy activities.

There is no reference to date to policy coherence for development in Iceland's legal or policy frameworks, partly because Iceland has a very limited development footprint in the world's poorest countries. Nevertheless, domestic implementation of the 2030 Agenda offers an opportunity for Iceland to examine the impact of its policies on developing countries. Experience from the OECD shows that the centre of government is the right place to address policy coherence for development and Iceland's choice to steer the domestic implementation of the 2030 Agenda through the Prime Minister's Office is likely to help it recognise if, and how, its policies impact negatively on developing countries and to improve its capacity to identify solutions.

Iceland recognises the value of aid as a catalyst for development finance and the role that the private sector can play in achieving the Sustainable Development Goals. In reflecting on how to strengthen its efforts in these areas in its new policy for development co-operation, Iceland could build upon the areas where it has a comparative advantage and which have most potential to offer long-term benefits for sustainable development. For example, Iceland is well-known for its technical expertise and multi-stakeholder partnerships, particularly in geothermal energy. In deepening this work with the private sector, however, the small size of Iceland's development administration must also be considered.

Recommendations

1.1 As Iceland discusses its response to the Sustainable Development Goals at home, it needs to promote, in a light-touch manner, better understanding of policy trade-offs across government, including any impacts in developing countries.

1.2 In reflecting on how to deepen and strengthen its work with the private sector, Iceland could draw upon its experience working with geothermal energy actors, an area which speaks to its comparative advantage as a donor.

2 Iceland's vision and policies for development co-operation

Indicator: Clear political directives, policies and strategies shape the member's development co-operation and are in line with international commitments and guidance

Main findings

With more than three decades experience as a bilateral donor prior to joining the DAC, Iceland has a long-standing focus on eradicating poverty in the world's poorest countries in line with international commitments. The main objective of Iceland's development co-operation is to support efforts by governments in developing countries to eradicate poverty and hunger and to promote economic and social development. This is anchored in Iceland's law and overarching strategy for development co-operation.

Iceland's development co-operation efforts are concentrated in least developed countries in Africa. In its development co-operation strategy 2013-16, Iceland sets out three clear priorities for its development co-operation efforts – natural resources, social infrastructure and peace-building – with gender and environment as cross-cutting issues. Within these broad themes, Iceland's specific efforts in areas such as geothermal energy align well with its established comparative advantage globally. In addition, in its bilateral partnerships with Malawi and Uganda, Iceland uses a district level approach to make its support to local communities more effective – focusing heavily on social sector support in health, education, water and sanitation, and local administration.

Furthermore, the recent integration of the former bilateral agency ICEIDA with the Ministry for Foreign Affairs is increasing the synergies between Iceland's development and foreign policy, strengthening alignment between bilateral and multilateral aid policy while also improving co-ordination between development co-operation and humanitarian assistance. As a result, Iceland's development programme has become even more focused, concentrating resources on priority themes and partners. This is improving Iceland's rationale for allocating its development assistance and the effectiveness of its programme.

There are, however, areas where Iceland could show a clearer alignment between its strategic objectives and programming. These include:

- The Reykjavik-based training programmes of the United Nations University, where the poverty focus and development impacts of the programmes are yet to be established.

- Iceland's rationale for shifting allocations from fisheries' management to district-level programmes.

In 2015, an amendment to Iceland's development co-operation act mandated a new five-year development policy for 2017-21, to be accompanied by two-year rolling action plans. However, delays in forming a government following the 2016 national elections have deferred this new framework. When designing this new framework for its development co-operation, Iceland has an important opportunity to update its rationale for allocating aid and other resources across its development co-operation portfolio.

Iceland has a deliberate and careful way of looking at its cross-cutting issues of gender equality and the environment. More than 80% of its bilateral allocable aid is reported as targeting gender equality and women's empowerment – well above the DAC member average of 35%. A planned evaluation of gender will help Iceland understand the impacts of these mainstreaming activities to date and how to target future efforts. However, Iceland could make further efforts to improve the impact of environmental mainstreaming activities across its programme.

The development of a new policy could also assist Iceland to sharpen its focus on key partners and themes in line with its comparative advantage and re-examine the impacts of its programme on its core poverty and hunger objective. In doing so, Iceland will also need to clarify how its development co-operation will contribute to achieving the Sustainable Development Goals.

Recommendations

2.1 As Iceland develops its national plan for delivering on the 2030 Agenda and the institutional framework through which this will take place, it should clarify how development co-operation will be integrated into the plan.

2.2 As the Ministry for Foreign Affairs plans for a new development policy and rolling action plan for the period 2017-21, it should define criteria to prioritise activities in line with Iceland's poverty focus and comparative advantage. This should help to guide future selection of partners and funding instruments.

3 Allocating Iceland's official development assistance

Indicator: The member's international and national commitments drive aid volume and allocations

Main findings

In 2015, Iceland's official development assistance (ODA) stood at USD 40 million, equivalent to 0.24% of its gross national income (GNI), ranking it 28th by volume and 17th in terms of aid as a share of national income.

Iceland stands out among donors for the high proportion of aid going to the world's poorest countries. Four-fifths of its bilateral allocable ODA is spent in least developed countries, mostly in fragile states. This is double the average share of other DAC members in these countries. However, Iceland does not see itself as a fragile states donor, despite the concentration of its aid in countries which are classed as fragile. Instead, its choice of priority partner countries – Malawi, Mozambique and Uganda – reflects Iceland's commitment to allocate its aid where it is most needed and where it can best add value.

Iceland has a long-standing commitment to reach the UN's target of allocating 0.7% of its GNI as ODA. This commitment remains. However, Iceland's level of ambition diminished significantly in the wake of the financial crisis. Whereas it previously set 2019 as the year by which it would reach the 0.7% target, it is now planning for ODA to rise marginally to 0.26% of GNI by 2018 and to remain there until 2021.

While this cautious approach is understandable, current levels of ambition do not reflect Iceland's strong recovery and projected robust economic growth. Going forward, the government's five-year budgetary framework could well help plan for a gradual and sustained increase in ODA in line with economic growth.

In 2015, 78% of Iceland's ODA was provided bilaterally. The geographic allocation of bilateral ODA is consistent with its commitment to the poorest countries in sub-Saharan Africa. It concentrates on social infrastructure as well as areas where Iceland has forged a comparative advantage (e.g. gender equality and geothermal energy).

The composition of Iceland's bilateral ODA envelope is now changing as spending on refugees within Iceland increased from 1% in 2013 to 12% of Iceland's gross ODA in 2015. To date, the Althingi's approval of additional allocations of ISK 2 billion (USD 15 million) to meet these costs in 2015-16 has protected Iceland's ability to deliver on existing commitments within its programme. Iceland has thus succeeded in managing these costs without undermining aid predictability for partner countries – an area where it has a strong reputation.

Iceland is a valued partner for its priority multilateral organisations, with lean management processes and a reputation for flexible funding. In particular, Iceland is valued for its willingness to champion start-up initiatives on environmental sustainability and gender equality. In 2015, its core contributions to key multilateral partners grew by 47%, more than those of any other DAC member, although this was largely due to the change of payment schedule for Iceland's contribution to the World Bank's International Development Association.

Iceland's multilateral allocations target four priority partners, complement bilateral efforts and are generally aligned with its overall strategy. A possible exception is its support to United Nations University scholarship programmes within Iceland; an evaluation currently underway should help to identify how these allocations can better align with the goals of Iceland's development co-operation. Finally, Iceland's regional approach to geothermal energy in the East African Rift Valley draws on its domestic expertise, building partnerships for leverage and scale.

In 2015, as part of the integration of ICEDA into the Ministry for Foreign Affairs, Iceland introduced a new single budget line for development co-operation. This makes allocations for development co-operation across bilateral, multilateral and humanitarian portfolios more transparent and strengthens Iceland's ability to target assistance where it is most needed.

Recommendations

3.1 In line with Iceland's continued economic recovery and forecasts for robust economic growth, Iceland should increase its ODA in real terms, using its five-year budgetary framework to establish a more ambitious timeline for meeting its 0.7% UN ODA to GNI commitment.

3.2 Iceland should ensure that its Reykjavik-based scholarship programme aligns with the overarching poverty focus of its programme and that it achieves tangible development results.

4 Managing Iceland's development co-operation

Indicator: The member's approach to how it organises and manages its development co-operation is fit for purpose

Main findings

Since joining the DAC in 2013, Iceland has continued to strengthen its institutional framework to deliver quality development co-operation. In 2016, Iceland integrated its bilateral development agency, ICEIDA, within the Ministry for Foreign Affairs – meaning almost all of Iceland's bilateral and multilateral development co-operation activities are now managed within the ministry.

The merger aimed to increase the flexibility and improve the co-ordination of Iceland's system. Although it is too early to assess the full impact of the merger, bringing all development co-operation activities under one institution has improved the alignment of Iceland's foreign, trade and development co-operation policies. Importantly, the merger has already helped to build synergies across channels of delivery and approaches, while safeguarding Iceland's pre-merger commitments to partner countries.

Permanent, ad-hoc and informal structures for whole-of-government co-ordination are in place in Iceland. These structures allow for more systematic policy co-ordination and for leveraging relevant expertise on development-related matters when needed. Moreover, Iceland's new integrated structure for the administration of development co-operation activities is making such co-ordination an easier task – which in turn is making Iceland's development co-operation more flexible and pragmatic.

An important aspect of the new integrated setup is that Iceland's embassies in Malawi, Mozambique and Uganda receive only one direction from headquarters. Iceland's Ambassador to these countries also heads its Directorate of International Development Cooperation in the Ministry for Foreign Affairs. In addition, the new single budget line for development funding simplifies the process of resource allocations across channels. As a result, Iceland has reduced transaction costs while increasing the effectiveness of its decision-making processes and flexibility of its funding.

The 2016 reform of Iceland's development co-operation committees, whose membership and competencies had been overlapping, has strengthened its advisory system. Iceland's single new Committee on International Development Cooperation has a stronger mandate and broader composition, which usefully brings together key development co-operation stakeholders and is improving awareness and understanding of development co-operation in Iceland's Althingi.

Despite its pragmatic and flexible approach, and adaption to new circumstances and reform, Iceland still needs to give time for the merger to filter through, so as to ensure that the reform bears long-lasting results. To support this process, Iceland will need to finalise its organisational structure (and corresponding unit functions) and continue reflecting on how to harmonise career incentives and staff conditions of service.

Staffing levels fell as a result of Iceland's economic crisis and cuts to its development co-operation budget. Staff levels have now stabilised, but there is awareness that capacity needs to grow in specific areas (e.g. humanitarian assistance, global public goods, results management, and fragile states). Encouragingly, development co-operation staff have received training in results-based management and evaluation to support implementation of Iceland's development policy and improve the quality of Iceland's aid programme.

There is scope for Iceland's Ministry for Foreign Affairs to integrate the specific needs of the development co-operation programme into its broader human resource management. The integration of all development co-operation activities under the ministry risks diluting development expertise through the ministry's staff rotation system, exacerbated by the lack of tailor-made training on development for all diplomats. At the same time, the merger provides an opportunity for the Ministry to make more staff aware of development-related activities.

Recommendations

4.1 As it consolidates the merger of its bilateral agency with its Ministry for Foreign Affairs, Iceland should review the implementation of its recent reforms to ensure that it remains a responsive, flexible and high-quality development co-operation provider.

4.2 The Ministry for Foreign Affairs should take care to retain staff with development co-operation expertise through careful planning of rotations, promotional opportunities and focusing on future training needs for both development professionals and diplomats.

5 Iceland's development co-operation delivery and partnerships

Indicator: The member's approach to how it delivers its programme leads to quality assistance in partner countries, maximizing the impact of its support, as defined in Busan

Main findings

Iceland's strategy for development co-operation (2013-16) provides an overarching framework for providing effective development co-operation, in line with the Paris, Accra and Busan commitments.

Iceland monitors progress on a number of these commitments and has been improving its performance over time. Iceland makes good use of district-level systems, is well aligned with national and district development priorities, co-ordinates with other donors in a meaningful way, and unties all of its aid.

Iceland is making its programming and budgeting processes more predictable and flexible through a new rolling five-year budgetary framework. In addition, Iceland also uses input targets for humanitarian and multilateral core contributions, which aims to avoid large deviations from stated priorities and to provide greater predictability for its partners.

Bilateral embassies also have a degree of flexibility in their operations, with the possibility of reallocating up to 10% of their budget within programmes. Such flexibility is commendable, especially given that the fragile contexts in which Iceland operates may require funds to be re-programmed at short notice.

Since 2012, Iceland's bilateral activities have adopted a programmatic approach, starting in Malawi and then in Uganda. In these programmes, Iceland emphasises building the capacity of district stakeholders, transferring responsibilities to district-level partners to provide essential social services (health, water and sanitation, education) and fostering local ownership. Iceland shares its lessons with other donors working in its partner countries, which is good practice.

Iceland applies performance-based conditions to mitigate risks in its district activities. These conditions are mutually agreed and based on clear requirements, which translates into better development outcomes. Notwithstanding this, Iceland and its partners could reflect on how to ensure greater national-level buy-in to ensure investments at district level endure beyond the life of the programme.

Iceland co-ordinates with other donors – in particular Nordic donors – to maximise the impact of its limited resources. Iceland also has strong partnerships with a range of development actors. The regional geothermal energy programme in the East African Rift Valley is a good illustration of Iceland's ability to make the most of its expertise and local knowledge through a partnership for leverage and scale-up.

Iceland has strong relations with civil society, especially Icelandic organisations working in the humanitarian domain. Iceland plans to scale up such partnerships in the future, including by working more with civil society groups in partner countries. In the meantime, Iceland has been streamlining its procedures for working with and funding civil society organisations and is in the process of implementing framework agreements.

To enhance its work with civil society organisations, Iceland could further reflect on the added value of this type of work. Doing so would help Iceland build upon the comparative advantages of these organisations, while raising awareness of development co-operation domestically. In doing so, Iceland could capitalise on the stronger mandate of its new Committee on International Development Cooperation to advise, to provide oversight, to increase awareness of, and to improve transparency in Iceland's development co-operation activities.

Iceland does not have an overarching strategy for engaging in crisis contexts. However, it does have very solid strategies for crisis management in Afghanistan and the Middle East. These strategies could provide a good basis for a policy on crisis management, which would help to ensure alignment between the overall objectives of Iceland's development co-operation and its work in crisis-affected areas.

Recommendations

5.1 The Ministry for Foreign Affairs could use its existing country strategies in crisis-affected areas to develop clear and consistent policy directives for crisis management across Iceland's development programme.

5.2 The Ministry for Foreign Affairs should make clear its strategic vision and rationale for selecting civil society partners. It could also improve guidance on how to work with these partners.

6. Results management and accountability of Iceland's development co-operation

Indicator: The member plans and manages for results, learning, transparency and accountability

Main findings

Iceland is planning to improve links between results and funding decisions across its development co-operation programme. This is driven by a 2015 amendment to its development co-operation act which provides for a more joined-up approach to development results reporting and more active parliamentary oversight by the Althingi.

The amendment provides for a new approach to results management in Iceland's expected 2017-21 policy on development co-operation and accompanying action plan. This places greater emphasis on commitment to, and alignment with, the Sustainable Development Goals and discussions. Moreover, all line ministries in Iceland must submit a "results framework" to the Finance Ministry as a part of the new five-year Statement of Fiscal Policy and Fiscal Strategy Plan for the public sector. The Directorate for International Development Cooperation is a separate expenditure area and will be held accountable for its results through the budget approval process.

In designing its new action plan, Iceland should continue to improve how it measures outcomes for development results. It should also reflect on how to measure results at country level in a way that can align with core strategic objectives. This does not mean trying to directly attribute Iceland's local-level efforts in the achievement of the global goals. Rather, it implies demonstrating commitment to – and alignment with – those goals prioritised by partners as part of Iceland's overall effort.

Iceland is strengthening its evaluation culture, using evaluations for evidence-based decision making and accountability. From the outset of a programme, reviews (internal and external) and external evaluations are planned for, funded and shared by partners to strengthen mutual accountability and promote learning.

While Iceland does not regularly commission impact evaluations, those it has undertaken have shown positive and sustainable impacts for the poorest after Icelandic aid ended. When evaluations show poor results, the flexible, transparent and pragmatic nature of Iceland's programming helps it to change course quickly, minimising harm and maximising opportunities.

The release of Iceland's 2016 evaluation policy presents a new opportunity to extend Iceland's learning on evaluation to multilateral, humanitarian and civil society partners. In addition to extending knowledge, the policy should also help Iceland to improve evaluation planning, safeguard the independence of the evaluations themselves and ensure they adhere to the DAC's best practice guidance on evaluation.

Iceland is a transparent donor, committed to regularly publishing programme information on its website. However, surveys show that despite high public support for development co-operation, public knowledge about Iceland's efforts is poor. With a new external Committee on International Development Cooperation in place, and an updated development communication strategy, Iceland has the necessary tools to improve awareness of – and accountability for – its development co-operation programme. In doing so, Iceland could make better use of country-based evidence on development impact and the global goals as key entry points to improve public and political awareness of Iceland's international development work.

Recommendations

6.1 In its new policy and action plan for development co-operation, Iceland should develop a more comprehensive approach to managing for results at the strategic, programme and activity levels, aligning with the Sustainable Development Goals and partner government frameworks.

6.2 Iceland should use its Committee on International Development Co-operation and new media platforms to improve public and political awareness of its development results, using annual public opinion surveys as a measure for success.

7 Iceland's humanitarian assistance

Indicator: The member contributes to minimising impact of shocks and crises; and saves lives, alleviates suffering and maintains human dignity in crisis and disaster settings

Main findings

Iceland's humanitarian strategy is driven by international humanitarian law and the Good Humanitarian Donorship principles. Iceland is also following the evolution of global humanitarian policy, including through commitments at the 2016 World Humanitarian Summit. Iceland intends, for example, to increase its support to humanitarian pooled funds, to add to its predictable core or lightly earmarked funding to its multilateral partners. As such, Iceland is a good system player in the UN-led humanitarian architecture.

Iceland approved a supplementary, allocation for 2015-16 to address the Syrian refugee crisis; this indicates good capacity to match strategic objectives with adequate resources, and also fosters co-ordination between relevant ministries within the government.

Iceland actively co-ordinates with other donors, taking advantage of its membership of the Nordic donor group and the Nordic plus group to reinforce its messages to its multilateral partners. Iceland's strategic focus on gender equality throughout its humanitarian and development programming helps create coherence between these different instruments.

Iceland complements its limited humanitarian funds by seconding technical experts to its partner UN humanitarian agencies' missions, via standby partnership agreements. This is a good way for Iceland to increase its involvement and visibility in crisis management and humanitarian action.

Iceland is helping build the resilience of vulnerable populations through support to social sectors at district level. While this provides an opportunity to strengthen sub-national systems, sustainability remains an issue. Iceland should ensure its development co-operation investment is sustained by government ownership and appropriate national funding. This will help ensure an effective transition and avoid over-dependence on long-term humanitarian support.

Iceland has a range of reasons for engaging in crisis contexts. These include its membership of the North Atlantic Treaty Organization (NATO) and the Organisation for Security and Co-operation in Europe (OSCE) and its role in responding to the current refugee crisis. In such contexts, Iceland uses a range of crisis management instruments from humanitarian aid to development and peacebuilding missions. However, there are no overarching guiding principles or strategies for engaging in individual crises, which reduces the potential for synergies among the various Icelandic programmes.

The merger between ICEIDA and the Ministry for Foreign Affairs creates an opportunity to better link humanitarian action, development co-operation and peacebuilding in crisis areas. In the new setup, the Icelandic Crisis Response Unit (ICRU) has yet to find its role. Created for security expert deployment in international missions, it is now under the responsibility of the Directorate for Development Co-operation and is also used to deploy humanitarian expertise in crisis areas. The ICRU has already proven its effectiveness in managing a range of peacebuilding humanitarian deployments to crisis countries. Given the inter-twined nature of humanitarian, security and development issues in current crisis environments, and in order to promote a streamlined structure for crisis response, Iceland should consider whether the ICRU could usefully serve as the official co-ordinating body in future. This reflection should be informed by the evaluation of past crisis responses.

Recommendation

7.1 Iceland should designate a single co-ordination mechanism for responses in crisis-affected countries, giving due consideration to existing structures, for example the ICRU.

Secretariat's report

Chapter 1: Towards a comprehensive Icelandic development effort

Global development issues

Iceland contributes to the global development agenda in a strategic and joined-up manner. In doing so, Iceland takes a selective approach, advocating for gender equality, renewable energy, sustainable fisheries, and land restoration. These are areas where Iceland has forged an international reputation and where its knowledge can have global benefit. In its work to shape the 2030 Agenda for Sustainable Development, Iceland uses its diplomatic weight to promote global public goods.

Iceland uses its diplomatic influence well to address key risks and shape global development policy in areas where it can make a difference

Iceland is a committed member of the international community, contributing to the global development agenda in a focused and strategic way. It provides and manages global public goods in those areas that play to its strengths: gender equality, geothermal energy, fisheries and land restoration. These priorities permeate Iceland's foreign policy and partnerships.

In 2015, Iceland was actively engaged in the international processes leading up to: (i) the 2030 Agenda for Sustainable Development and the Sustainable Development Goals; (ii) the Addis Ababa Action Agenda on Financing for Development; and (iii) the Paris Agreement on climate change, which Iceland ratified early on thus promoting its entry into force in 2016 (Ministry for Foreign Affairs, 2016). In these processes, Iceland championed, led discussions and advocated for its chosen focus areas. For example, it vocally supported the inclusion of sexual and reproductive health and rights, the treatment of neurological disorders and respect for lesbian, gay, bisexual and transsexual rights in the 2030 Agenda.

Iceland also financed the participation in climate negotiations of civil society organisations working on gender issues and emphasised the prevention and treatment of neurological disorders in line with a Parliamentary Resolution adopted in 2014. Iceland also advocated for separate Sustainable Development Goals on gender equality, renewable energy and oceans and for gender to be mainstreamed across all goals (see Box 1.1), as well as specific targets on sexual and reproductive health and rights. In addition, it co-founded the group of friends on desertification, land degradation and drought to raise awareness of related matters in the climate change negotiations and the 2030 Agenda process.

Iceland uses its role in international fora to develop partnerships to support shared global outcomes. For example, in 2011 Iceland launched a geothermal compact with the World Bank, which it implements in co-operation with the Nordic Development Fund, to support 13 developing countries in the East African Rift Valley in harnessing their geothermal energy resources (Box 5.2, Chapter 5; Government of Iceland and Nordic Development Fund, 2012). Iceland also uses its position well as a member of key multilateral and regional organisations to achieve greater influence. This was demonstrated by Iceland's contribution to improving gender equality and gender mainstreaming in the work of the World Bank (Ministry for Foreign Affairs, 2011).

However, Iceland recognises that there is room to improve how it tackles key global challenges, such as climate change mitigation, and how it communicates and explains to the public its efforts to implement these issues at home.

> **Box 1.1. Iceland's advocacy for gender**
>
> Iceland has stepped up its international policy advocacy on issues related to gender equality. Of particular note was Iceland's leadership in championing gender issues in the Sustainable Development Goals and financing for development processes, and at the United Nations Commission on the Status of Women. In 2015, Iceland hosted an informal meeting of interested DAC members to develop common proposals on gender equality ahead of the final intergovernmental negotiations on the 2030 Agenda and the Third International Conference on Financing for Development. Iceland (and its former Prime Minister in particular) has also been an active supporter of the UN Women's "He for She Campaign", which aims to engage men and boys in challenging inequality and discrimination faced by women and girls. In addition, Iceland organised and supported various "Barbershop Conferences" to rally men and boys to uphold gender equality.
>
> *Source:* Interviews in Reykjavik (September 2016); information provided by the Secretariat of the DAC Network on Gender Equality (2016); Ministry for Foreign Affairs (2013), Strategy for Iceland's International Development Cooperation (2013-2016), www.mfa.is/media/throunarsamvinna/MFA-StrategyforIcelandsDevelopmentCooperation-2013-2016.pdf.

Policy coherence for development
Indicator: Domestic policies support or do not harm developing countries

Iceland has a limited development footprint in the world's poorest countries and a small administration. Even so, Iceland is taking steps towards more development-friendly domestic policies in the areas of climate change and foreign bribery. However, while it has formal and informal co-ordination mechanisms to address policy coherence for development in its external action, Iceland does not yet have a system or the capacity to systematically screen domestic policies or identify priority issues. A focal point has been recently nominated at the Ministry for Foreign Affairs. This could help Iceland analyse more thoroughly how its domestic policies may affect developing countries.

Iceland is committed to policy coherence for development

Iceland is one of the world's most sparsely populated countries and has one of the smallest domestic economies in the world. Iceland's trade relations with developing countries, although growing in recent years, make up a small share of its international trade (WTO, 2012). Likewise, Iceland only has a small development footprint in poor countries.

As a member of the OECD, Iceland has endorsed the OECD Ministerial Declaration on Policy Coherence for Development (OECD, 2008), which aims to foster synergies across policy areas (e.g. environment, agriculture, fisheries, trade, and migration) in a way that supports or does no harm to developing country aspirations. However, there is no reference to policy coherence for development in Iceland's legal or policy framework.

Iceland has recently nominated a staff member in the Ministry for Foreign Affairs as a policy coherence focal point. This is an opportunity to develop a more strategic approach that identifies those key policy issues where greater coherence is required. It should help Iceland to better address its international commitments in the future.

Chapter 1: Towards a comprehensive Icelandic development effort

The Sustainable Development Goals offer an opportunity to improve policy coherence for development

Iceland is still defining the mandate of the recently created focal point in the Ministry for Foreign Affairs. As a result, it has not yet systematically analysed, monitored or reported on progress to make its domestic policies more development-friendly. Iceland's efforts to date have focused on co-ordinating its external action rather than on addressing how domestic policies might affect its partners – understandably, given the small size of its economy and its limited potential development impact.

The Ministry for Foreign Affairs is involved in development-related processes led by other line ministries. The Minister for Foreign Affairs participates when relevant in the Ministerial Standing Committee on Inter-Ministerial Co-ordination, which includes the Prime Minister and the Minister for Finance. Issues that require inter-ministerial co-ordination are usually submitted to the Standing Committee and officials from the ministry are involved in this work. Ad-hoc inter-ministerial committees can also be set up to co-ordinate development-related issues more formally, as needed. These committees can deal with policy coherence for development issues. For example, in 2015 the Prime Minister's Office and the ministries for Foreign Affairs, Welfare and the Interior created a committee to deal with the international asylum and refugee crisis. The ministries for Foreign Affairs and Environment co-ordinate Iceland's climate-related commitments, ahead of climate negotiations, which are then implemented domestically.

Iceland is currently working on its architecture for implementing the Sustainable Development Goals. This is led by the Prime Minister's Office in close co-operation with the Ministry for Foreign Affairs. The office is already considering how its domestic policies might align with the Sustainable Development Goals. This presents an opportunity for Iceland to identify, analyse, monitor and report cases of incoherence. This architecture will need to be compatible with the mandate of the newly created policy coherence focal point and other ad hoc committees; while development-related issues will need to be included in any domestic plan to implement these goals.

Iceland could use all the mechanisms described above, including the policy coherence focal point, to ensure that policy trade-offs are systematically assessed in the Ministry for Foreign Affairs and other line ministries. In doing so, Iceland could also make greater use of models from other OECD countries to design formal mechanisms and analytical tools to address domestic policies that are harmful to developing countries (OECD, 2016a). The focal point could also play a pivotal role in the trade policy measures that Iceland is currently envisioning and that aim to benefit low-income countries.

Iceland's policies for climate and combating foreign bribery are more development friendly

Iceland has analysed the benefits of coherence in some areas. For example, its gender-responsive budgeting mandates that government budget proposals must be gender-responsive and should be screened for their impact on women's rights in accordance with national and international provisions. Another example is Iceland's implementation of the OECD's Convention on Combating Bribery of Foreign Public Officials in International Business Transactions (OECD, 2010). A recent assessment of Iceland's progress in implementing the convention found that despite some initial difficulties, it is working to incorporate anti-corruption clauses in government contracts and to review -- in line with the OECD's recommendations (OECD, 2013) – the Code of Conduct that the Ministry for Foreign Affairs adopted in 2009.

While Iceland has a small impact on development in developing countries, it is exercising leadership by recognising that it needs to make some of its policies more development-friendly, as is the case for many other DAC members. For example, Iceland is

Chapter 1: Towards a comprehensive Icelandic development effort

aware that its international status as an industrialised economy running only on renewable energy does not sit well with its high energy footprint, both per capita and per unit of gross domestic product, in sectors that contribute to climate change (e.g. agriculture or transport; OECD, 2014; Kroll, 2016). Iceland has nevertheless made progress in mainstreaming climate-related issues domestically and, jointly with the European Union and Norway, aims to cut its greenhouse gas emissions by 40% in 2030 (from a 1990 baseline), including in the fisheries and agricultural sectors (OECD, 2016b).

Financing for development
Indicator: The member engages in development finance in addition to ODA

Iceland interprets catalytic funding differently from other DAC providers and does not have a formal strategy for promoting ODA as a catalyst to attract additional resources. However, it does engage in activities that can leverage domestic and private resources in partner countries, notably its regional delivery model and its international policy advocacy. Iceland's financing for multilateral organisations promotes innovative projects that can attract further funds from other providers. Iceland does not report on non-ODA flows as it does not have non-ODA financial instruments.

Iceland recognises the value of aid as a catalyst but does not have a strategy to leverage non-ODA development finance

Iceland recognises the need for non-ODA development finance and the role that aid can play to catalyse private investment in development in partner countries. However, Iceland has no overall strategy to leverage non-ODA development finance or to promote the role of aid as a catalyst for private investment in development. This is understandable – Iceland's small private sector footprint in developing countries means that its capacity to blend aid with other finance is limited. Even so, Iceland is considering how it can better link its ODA to other forms of development finance for sustainable results.

For example, Iceland views its grant-based aid to developing countries as catalytic in the sense that it supports sustainable investments in health, water and education. This, in turn, builds human capital in local communities and increases their capacity to attract other providers of development co-operation and private finance. Iceland also views its regional grants to the East African Rift Valley Geothermal Energy Project as catalytic: by aiming to mitigate and distribute the risks associated with geothermal exploration, it clears many bottlenecks to private sector investment (high exploration costs, high drilling and reservoir risks, and long development times) (see Box 5.2, Chapter 5).

Iceland backs up its policy advocacy in priority areas with seed finance to multilateral organisations. This helps catalyse financing from other providers and is valued by organisations such as the United Nations Entity for Gender Equality and the Empowerment of Women (UN WOMEN) and the UN Children's Fund (UNICEF). In addition, Iceland supports the implementation of financial mechanisms to mitigate climate change in accordance with the objectives of the Green Climate Fund, to which it has pledged an unearmarked grant of USD 1 million (GCF, 2016). Iceland also advocated strongly for domestic resource mobilisation during the 2015 Addis Ababa Conference on Financing for Development.

Chapter 1: Towards a comprehensive Icelandic development effort

Iceland could begin a dialogue with the private sector involved in developing countries

Iceland has no official financial instruments, such as guarantees or export credits, for leveraging private investment in developing countries, and has no plans to start using such instruments. All of Iceland's ODA is provided in grant form.

Iceland's capacity for engaging in development co-operation with the domestic private sector is low; to date, apart from one entrepreneurship programme in Uganda, it has not prioritised working or partnering with the private sector, such as through co-financing or subsidising pro-poor business activities. Although Iceland's private sector would like to engage more with developing countries, the government will need greater capacity if it is to work with the private sector – in particular with the geothermal energy sector, where its engagement with the private sector shows strongest potential.

Building on Iceland's emerging experience using ODA to catalyse private investment in development in partner countries, such as through the geothermal energy project in East Africa, Iceland could explore potential for new work with the private sector through a light-touch dialogue to share development-related good practice and better understand companies' activities in developing countries. This dialogue could build on existing links between the Ministry for Foreign Affairs' Directorate for International Development Cooperation and industry-wide clusters on geothermal energy or fisheries. Discussions are already underway with the geothermal cluster and geothermal companies involved. These clusters can be entry points for discussing development issues with representatives from the private sector and other government agencies.

Iceland does not track or report on non-ODA flows

Limited administrative capacity means that Iceland does not yet track or report on other official flows, private grants (funds raised by non-governmental organisations and foundations) or private flows at market terms from Iceland to developing countries.

There are some government-funded activities to develop the trade capacity of developing countries, principally technical co-operation through the European Free Trade Association Secretariat, to which Iceland supplies experts on request. In addition, Iceland makes some of the largest private contributions in per capita terms (funds raised by non-governmental organisations and foundations) to two of its priority multilateral organisations, UN Women and UNICEF. The contributions from the Icelandic national committees of these organisations represented 40% of the total Icelandic contribution to UN Women and 57% to UNICEF in 2014 (the rest being ODA flows) (UNICEF 2015; UN Women 2016). In both cases, when considering both types of flows (ODA and private), Iceland is the fourth biggest donor in per capita terms.

Chapter 1: Towards a comprehensive Icelandic development effort

Bibliography

Government sources

Government of Iceland and Nordic Development Fund (2012), *East African Rift Valley Geothermal Exploration Project (2013-2017)*, Government of Iceland, Reykjavik.

ICEIDA (2012), *Guiding Principles for Addressing Environmental Issues*, Icelandic International Development Agency, Reykjavik, www.iceida.is/media/pdf/Guiding-Principles-for-Environmental-Issues.pdf.

MFA (2016), "Iceland ratifies the Paris Agreement", press release, Ministry for Foreign Affairs, Reykjavik, www.mfa.is/news-and-publications/nr/8919.

MFA (2013), *Strategy for Iceland's International Development Cooperation (2013-2016)*, www.mfa.is/media/throunarsamvinna/MFA-StrategyforIcelandsDevelopmentCooperation-2013-2016.pdf.

MFA (2011), *Overview of Iceland's Development Cooperation 2009-10*, Ministry for Foreign Affairs, Reykjavik, www.mfa.is/media/throunarsamvinna/Icelands_International_Development_Cooperation_MFA-ICEIDA.pdf.

MFA and ICEIDA (2013), *Gender Equality Policy for Iceland's Development Cooperation*, Ministry for Foreign Affairs and Icelandic International Development Agency, Reykjavik, www.mfa.is/media/throunarsamvinna/UTR-GenderEquality-2013.pdf.

Other sources

GCF (2016), Status of Pledges and Contributions made to the Green Climate Fund, September 2016, Green Climate Fund, www.greenclimate.fund/partners/contributors/resources-mobilized.

Kroll, C. (2016), "Sustainable Development Goals: Are the rich countries ready?", Sustainable Governance Indicators, SDSN and Bertelsmann Stiftung, www.bertelsmann-stiftung.de/en/publications/publication/did/sustainable-development-goals-are-the-rich-countries-ready/.

OECD (2016a), Better Policies for Sustainable Development 2016: A New Framework for Policy Coherence, OECD Publishing, http://dx.doi.org/10.1787/9789264256996-en.

OECD (2016b), Agricultural Policy Monitoring and Evaluation 2016, OECD Publishing, http://dx.doi.org/10.1787/agr_pol-2016-en.

OECD (2014), OECD Environmental Performance Reviews: Iceland 2014, OECD Publishing, http://dx.doi.org/10.1787/9789264214200-en.

OECD (2013), Iceland: Follow-up to the Phase 3 Report and Recommendations, OECD, Paris, www.oecd.org/daf/anti-bribery/Icelandphase3writtenfollowupreportEN.pdf.

OECD (2010), Phase 3 Report on implementing the OECD Anti-bribery Convention in Iceland, OECD, Paris www.oecd.org/iceland/Icelandphase3reportEN.pdf.

OECD (2008), Ministerial Declaration on Policy Coherence for Development, OECD, Paris, www.oecd.org/pcd/ministerialdeclarationonpolicycoherencefordevelopment.htm.

UNICEF (2015), Annual Report 2015, UNICEF, New York, www.unicef.org/publications/index_92018.html.

UN Women (2016), Annual Report 2015-2016, UN Women, New York, http://annualreport.unwomen.org/~/media/annual%20report/attachments/sections/library/un-women-annual-report-2015-2016-en.pdf.

WTO (2012), Trade Policy Review: Iceland, World Trade Organization, Geneva, www.wto.org/english/tratop_e/tpr_e/tp373_e.htm.

Chapter 2: Iceland's vision and policies for development co-operation

Policies, strategies and commitments
Indicator: A clear policy vision and solid strategies guide the programme

In line with its international commitments, Iceland's development co-operation focuses on eradicating poverty and improving living standards in the world's poorest countries. The new hierarchy between Iceland's updated law, draft development co-operation policy and forthcoming action plan is developing well, with increasing synergies between development and foreign policy.

A clear focus on eradicating poverty and increasing synergies between development and foreign policies

Iceland has a clear focus on eradicating poverty in the world's poorest countries in line with its international commitments.[1]

This vision is anchored in Iceland's updated development co-operation act[2] (Althingi, 2015), which embeds development as a key pillar of Iceland's foreign policy. The act designates the Minister for Foreign Affairs as the supreme authority for Iceland's development co-operation. An external Development Cooperation Committee – drawn from parliament, non-government organisations, academia and the private sector – provides overarching policy advice and monitors the implementation of Iceland's international development cooperation.[3] The Committee meets at least twice a year with the Minister for Foreign Affairs and informs the Foreign Affairs Committee on its work.

The December 2015 amendment to the act abolished ICEIDA (the Icelandic International Development Agency), integrating all the agency's functions into the Ministry for Foreign Affairs.[4] The agency was previously responsible for implementing 40% of Iceland's official development assistance through bilateral programmes, while the ministry was responsible for the remaining 60% through multilateral co-operation. In addition to increasing links between development and foreign policy (Chapter 4), the integration of agency staff into the ministry is strengthening alignment between bilateral and multilateral aid policy while also improving co-ordination between development co-operation and humanitarian assistance.[5]

The updated act now provides a solid framework for the whole of Iceland's development co-operation – from bilateral and multilateral assistance, to humanitarian aid and conflict resolution activities. The goal of Iceland's international development co-operation is to support efforts by governments in developing countries to eradicate poverty and hunger and to promote economic and social development. Human rights, gender equality, peace and security are highlighted as key objectives, in conjunction with specific activities (such as fisheries and geothermal energy) that can draw on Iceland's domestic expertise.

This rationale is the backbone of Iceland's 2013-16 strategy (MFA, 2013). The strategy committed Iceland to the UN target of allocating 0.7% of its gross national income (GNI) as ODA. It also outlined an ambitious timeline for how to get there, with ODA scheduled to reach 0.42% of GNI by 2016 and 0.7% by 2019, joining neighbouring countries that have reached or surpassed this target. This trajectory has now been revised significantly

Chapter 2: Iceland's vision and policies for development co-operation

downwards, with Iceland's ODA standing at 0.24% of GNI in 2015, with the aim that the ratio will rise to 0.26% in 2018 and remain at this level until 2021 (Chapter 3). However, Iceland's underlying commitment to the UN's 0.7% goal remains and is referenced in the Ministry for Foreign Affairs' explanatory note accompanying Iceland's 2017 budget law (MFA, 2016).

Following the appointment of its new government in January 2017, Iceland is now due to formulate a new five-year development co-operation policy and associated action plan, as mandated through amendments to the act in December 2015. This would bring Iceland's development policy in line with its new five-year fiscal policy framework, on which its annual budget bill is based (Government of Iceland, 2016).

Overall, the hierarchy between Iceland's development co-operation law and the strategic framework for implementing its development co-operation is developing well and is helping to provide Iceland with a solid basis for pursuing the Sustainable Development Goals in a way that plays to its strengths. However, in the future, Iceland will need clear positions on how it intends to implement the Sustainable Development Goals, private sector partnerships and policy coherence for development. For this reason, Iceland would benefit from a clearer narrative for how top-level objectives link these to thematic and geographical priorities. A key lesson from other DAC peer reviews is that donors should focus their assistance on a few countries, a few sectors and, in particular, a few activities.

This is particularly important for donors with limited resources.

Approach to allocating bilateral and multilateral aid

Indicator: The rationale for allocating aid and other resources is clear and evidence-based

Iceland's strategy for development co-operation focuses allocations on fewer countries and multilateral partners. However, Iceland could further clarify its rationale for selecting partner countries and improving coherence between multilateral and bilateral aid priorities.

Iceland's bilateral programme is more focused geographically, but its rationale for allocating aid has not kept pace with shifting priorities

Iceland has a flexible and pragmatic approach to allocating bilateral aid. The overarching priority for Iceland's aid during the last strategy period (2013-16) was to support sustainable development and human development, with a particular focus on natural resources, social sector services (health and education) and crisis management. Within these priority areas, Iceland aims to focus its assistance on areas for which it has the knowledge and competence to share with developing countries, such as geothermal energy, sustainable fisheries and gender equality. This is particularly evident in Iceland's regional approach to geothermal energy in East Africa's Rift Valley, which draws on Iceland's comparative advantage in this area (Box 5.2 Chapter 5; MFA, 2013).

However, delays in forming a government in the wake of the 2016 election deferred plans to adopt a new development policy and associated action plan for 2017, leaving a gap in Iceland's strategic direction on aid policy and the 2030 Agenda for Sustainable Development. Iceland concentrates its bilateral support on three priority country partners – Malawi, Mozambique and Uganda – all of which are defined as least developed countries (Annex C).[6] Five criteria for country selection are outlined in ICEIDA's procedural guidance: poverty, population, low aid per capita, a peaceful context and improving governance (ICEIDA, 2011). In addition, Iceland notes in its memorandum to the DAC that

Chapter 2: Iceland's vision and policies for development co-operation

partner countries are selected on the basis of developmental needs, logistical and practical criteria and the track record of Icelandic aid in these contexts (Government of Iceland, 2016).

Historically, Iceland has selected partner countries based on their need for support in fisheries and renewable energy (ICEIDA, 2012a). However, as the programme has evolved, this sectoral focus has been subject to change, with support shifting to social infrastructure, particularly health and education programmes at district level. On one hand, this demonstrates Iceland's ability to respond flexibly and pragmatically to changing contexts and partner needs. But on the other, it weakens the logic for Iceland's comparative advantage in development co-operation set out in the 2013-16 strategy. This disconnect could be effectively remedied with the release of a new overarching policy in which social infrastructure (education, health, water and sanitation) are featured as entry points for Iceland's development co-operation based on its support for specific Sustainable Development Goals. Furthermore, forthcoming evaluations of the effectiveness of Iceland's work in these areas may contribute to the overarching rationale for how Iceland can add value in this sector at the district level (see Chapter 3).

In recent years, Iceland has reduced the number of its partner countries from five to three and is now considering how it can further concentrate its bilateral and multilateral programmes. As a result, reducing the number of individual activities would also be sensible given the likely small size of even an expanded Icelandic programme.

Iceland engages strategically with multilateral partners, in line with its policy

Iceland is committed to multilateralism and strongly supports multilateral approaches to solve key global challenges. Core and non-core multilateral allocations target four priority multilateral organisations – the United Nations University, UN Women, UNICEF and the World Bank – reflecting the emphasis of Iceland's overall strategy on gender equality, natural resources and environment. In addition, Iceland uses its participation in the governance arrangements of key multilateral partners strategically, focusing on geothermal energy, sustainable fisheries, land restoration and gender. As outlined in Annex C, this also creates positive synergies with Iceland's bilateral programmes. In its humanitarian programmes, Icelandic support for Afghanistan and the Middle East is also provided through multilateral partners. These allocations complement bilateral efforts, with Iceland providing increasing levels of core funding to help these organisations to fulfil their mandate. Bilateral allocations to multilateral partners (multi-bi aid) are concentrated on Iceland's three priority bilateral partners, as well as Afghanistan and the Middle East.

However, while Iceland's allocations to the four training programmes of the United Nations University (UNU) in Reykjavik are aligned with its strategic focus on fisheries, geothermal energy, land restoration and gender, it is not clear how these allocations contribute to Iceland's key objective of fighting poverty in developing countries (Box 2.1). In addition, the Development Assistance Committee's guidance on development capacity building notes that many members have reviewed their scholarship programmes and have found them not to be as cost-effective as other forms of capacity building (OECD, 2012). In recognition of this, some donors have moved away from scholarship programmes, focusing instead on in-country training and strengthening the capacity of training institutions in partner countries. The UNU delivery model established by the institution's headquarters in Tokyo is now evolving to provide more training and support for universities and research institutions in partner countries through twinning arrangements. However, while Iceland's programmes have begun to increase in-country training in recent years[7] in addition to the training provided in Iceland, there are no plans to adapt fully to the new model.

Chapter 2: Iceland's vision and policies for development co-operation

Therefore, the ongoing review of this programme's outcomes and impacts in developing countries is particularly timely. Measurement of country-level results will help Iceland to identify how these allocations can better align with, and contribute to, Iceland's overarching strategic development co-operation objectives. Furthermore, the potential financial impacts of the proposed new institutional arrangements will need to be carefully considered to ascertain whether this is an effective use of Iceland's ODA budget – in particular the higher overhead costs associated with the new layer of management and salary scales required in this new model by UNU headquarters in Tokyo (see Chapter 5).

Box 2.1 Iceland's support for the United Nations University in Reykjavik

The United Nations University's (UNU) four training programmes in Reykjavik are a top priority for Iceland's multilateral assistance, making up more than a quarter (26%) of Iceland's multilateral funding envelope. Since 1979, almost 1 000 developing country professionals have attended UNU training programmes, mostly through scholarships for six month post-graduate programmes funded by Iceland's official development assistance, with additional funding longer post-graduate scholarships in some cases.

In 2016, the unit cost for a student to attend one of the three half-year programmes in Reykjavik ranged from USD 31,000 for gender studies, USD 40,000 for geothermal energy, USD 45,000 for fisheries and USD 60,000 for land restoration. During six-month fellowships students conduct research, supervised by other researchers and academics, with development potential for their own countries or regions and using local data where possible. This is a sizeable investment in human capacity development, especially relative to other elements of Iceland's development co-operation (see Chapter 3). While the Iceland-based training programmes remain a core delivery model, in recent years the institution's headquarters in Tokyo has been promoting more training and support for universities and research institutions in partner countries through twinning arrangements. Increasingly, international scholarship beneficiaries also undertake research in home countries with financial support of UNU programmes.[8] Internal evaluations of the Reykjavik-based programmes show positive impacts on students and improved development data collection, as well as a high level of public support for the programmes in Iceland. However, there are no independent mechanisms in place to assure the quality of the programmes or to benchmark these impacts against similar programmes being run by other institutions. An external review, currently underway, will be the first evaluation of the overall impact of the programmes on fisheries, geothermal energy development or land restoration in the countries that have benefited from the training.

Sources: United Nations University website (https://unu.edu); and OECD (2013a), "Special Review of Iceland", www.oecd.org/dac/dac-global-relations/Iceland%20Special%20Review.pdf.

Policy focus

Indicator: Fighting poverty, especially in LDCs and fragile states, is prioritised

Iceland does not see itself as a fragile states donor, despite the concentration of its aid in least developed countries which are classed as fragile. However, there are increasing synergies between development and humanitarian aid in Iceland's development co-operation, reinforced by the new integrated structure in the Ministry for Foreign Affairs. This puts Iceland in a good position to implement a model that integrates humanitarian and development work, in line with its new government commitment to tackle the root causes of migration.

Chapter 2: Iceland's vision and policies for development co-operation

A focus on poverty has guided Iceland's programme

Reflecting its international commitments, Iceland has a clear focus on fighting poverty, improving living standards and reducing inequalities in the world's poorest countries. Iceland's *Strategy for International Development Cooperation 2013-16* is generally in line with DAC good practice and spells out its commitment to poverty reduction, aid effectiveness and international development obligations (MFA, 2013).

In 2015, almost half of Iceland's bilateral development assistance went to sub-Saharan Africa and 42% was allocated to least developed countries, far above the DAC average of 24%. Its choice of priority partner countries – Malawi, Mozambique and Uganda – reflects Iceland's commitment to assist the poorest. To sharpen this focus, Iceland aims to raise the proportion of the aid budget spent on least developed countries to around 50%, up from an average of 40% in 2015.

Development and humanitarian assistance are integrated into country programming in a coherent way

There are increasing synergies between development and humanitarian aid in Iceland's development co-operation (Chapter 7). This is underpinned by Iceland's strong commitment to applying the Good Humanitarian Donorship Principles (GHD 2003) in line with the outcomes of the World Humanitarian Summit. The new integrated structure for development co-operation is well suited to realising these linkages. However, much of the crisis management work is at the nexus between security and development. In its multilateral assistance in Afghanistan and the Middle East, Iceland operates through core allocations and secondments to UN agencies. However, the rationale for this work and how it aligns with Iceland's strengths could be better articulated in the strategic framework for its development co-operation.

Though Iceland works primarily in fragile states, it does not see itself as a fragile states donor

In its 2013-16 development co-operation strategy (MFA, 2013), Iceland highlights its motivation to support partnerships for peace and reconstruction in conflict-affected communities, especially fragile states. However, in its bilateral co-operation, Iceland focuses on least developed countries and states that are labelled as fragile but not in conflict. As such, although Iceland does not see itself as a fragile states donor, it is sensitive to conflict situations when deploying its development co-operation and humanitarian responses. However, while Iceland might not need a fragile states strategy, some form of guidance on how Iceland engages in crisis and conflict across its programme could help to reduce its risks in these environments and improve the quality of its development co-operation.

Gender and environmental sustainability are core values, but environmental mainstreaming is not fully analysed

Iceland has a deliberate and careful way of looking at its priority cross-cutting issues of gender equality and the environment, with more than 80% of its bilateral allocable aid reported as targeting gender equality and women's empowerment. This is well above the DAC member average of 35%.

Iceland also has a clear focus on gender in its multilateral work, with allocations for Afghanistan and the Middle East concentrated on gender. In working to improve systems for accountability and incentives for gender mainstreaming across its work, Iceland records results and disseminates lessons. In 2013, the former bilateral agency, ICEIDA, and the Ministry for Foreign Affairs released a joint Gender Equality Policy for the period 2013-2016. Following the integration of ICEDA and the Ministry for Foreign Affairs (see Chapter 4), gender tools designed by the former ICEIDA are now also benefitting the Ministry for Foreign Affair's gender mainstreaming efforts. A planned evaluation of gender will help Iceland understand the impacts of these mainstreaming activities to date and how to target future efforts.

However, Iceland could improve its understanding of the impact of its environmental mainstreaming activities across its programme. In addition to current mainstreaming efforts through strategic environmental assessment and environmental impact analyses, which Iceland routinely uses in its bilateral and regional activities, putting greater emphasis on reporting against the DAC's Rio markers that are part of the DAC's statistical reporting scoring system[9] would ensure even greater attention to environmental issues, as well as greater transparency on Iceland's level of support to environment and climate change objectives (ICEIDA, 2012).

Chapter 2: Iceland's vision and policies for development co-operation

Notes

1. Iceland's development co-operation effort goes back to 1971; Iceland was itself an aid recipient as recently as 1976.

2. Act No. 121/2008 on Iceland's development co-operation entered into force on 1 October 2008 (Althingi, 2008). It replaced previous legislation that committed Iceland to working towards a target of 1% ODA/GNI (Act No 20/1971) and established an autonomous development co-operation agency, ICEIDA, under the responsibility of the Ministry for Foreign Affairs with a mandate to promote co-operation between Iceland and developing countries. The founding act of ICEIDA (Act No 43/1981) included an objective of achieving 0.7% ODA/GNI.

3. The committee discusses the strategic and planning issues related to Iceland's international development cooperation, including budgetary allocations to ODA, choice of partner countries, Iceland's participation in the work of multilateral organisations and reports on results.

4. The integration meant all tasks of ICEIDA were moved into the Ministry for Foreign Affairs. Throughout this report, this organisational change will generally be referred to as a merger.

5. Two previous reviews (the DAC's 2013 Special Review of Iceland and a subsequent independent analysis) called for better co-ordination between ICEIDA and the Ministry for Foreign Affairs.

6. As defined by the United Nations Committee for Development Policy in its list of least developed countries, updated May 2016 (www.un.org/en/development/desa/policy/cdp/ldc/ldc_list.pdf).

7. The UNU's geothermal programme has carried out training in developing countries since the 1990s, mainly middle-income countries. For UNU more recent gender programme, work concentrates on least developed countries.

8. Spending in developing countries for UNU courses varies considerably across programs. For example, expenditure on the UNU's geothermal programme's short courses in Kenya and El Salvador in 2016 averaged USD 3 100 per student, while the UNU fisheries programme transferred USD 25 000 to students undertaking research in developing countries. These costs cannot be equated with the six-month training course in Iceland, as the benefits for developing countries of both types of courses are yet to be examined in the forthcoming evaluation of the development impacts of the UNU programmes in all four thematic areas.

9. The Rio Conventions on Climate Change, Biological Diversity and Desertification were established in 1992. Developed country parties committed to assist developing countries in the implementation of these conventions. The DAC established a scoring system based on three values, in which development co-operation activities are "marked" for the degree to which they target the environment or the Rio Conventions: as a "principal" objective or a "significant" objective, or as not targeting the objective. Five statistical policy markers exist to monitor external development finance for environmental purposes within the OECD/DAC: the "environment" marker and four Rio markers covering biodiversity, climate change adaptation, climate change mitigation and desertification. The Rio markers apply to official development assistance (ODA), and from 2010 have also applied to other official flows (non-concessional developmental flows, excluding export credits). See www.oecd.org/dac/environment-development/rioconventions.htm.

Chapter 2: Iceland's vision and policies for development co-operation

Bibliography

Government sources

Althingi (2015), *Amendment to Act No 121/2008 (Act 122/2015)*, entered into force January 2016, Althingi, Reykjavik.

Althingi (2012), *Amendment to Act No 121/2008 (Act 161/2012)*, enacted January 2013, Althingi, Reykjavik.

Althingi (2008), *Act on Iceland's International Development Co-operation (Act 121/2008)*, Althingi, Reykjavik, www.mfa.is/media/MFA_pdf/Act-on-Icelands-International-Development-Cooperation.pdf.

Government of Iceland (2016), "OECD DAC peer review of Iceland: memorandum", Government of Iceland, Reykjavik.

Government of Iceland (2011), *A Parliamentary Resolution on a Strategy for Iceland's International Development Co-operation 2011-2014*. Adopted by the Althingi 10 June 2011.

ICEIDA (2013), *Geothermal Exploration Project, NDF 2013-2017*, Icelandic International Development Agency, Reykjavik, www.iceida.is/iceida-projects/current-projects/nr/1488.

ICEIDA (2012), *Guiding Principles for Addressing Environmental Issues*, Icelandic International Development Agency, Reykjavik, www.iceida.is/media/pdf/Guiding-Principles-for-Environmental-Issues.pdf.

ICEIDA (2011), *Vision and Procedures 2012-2014*, Icelandic International Development Agency, Reykjavik, Reykjavik, www.iceida.is/media/pdf/Vision-and-Procedures-2012-2014.pdf.

MFA (2016), Explanatory note on development co-operation for Iceland's budget bill, adopted on 22 December 2016 (now the 2017 budget law). Ministry for Foreign Affairs, Reykjavik.

MFA (2013), *Strategy for Iceland's International Development Cooperation (2013-2016)*, (Icelandic only, highlights available in English), Ministry for Foreign Affairs, Reykjavik, www.mfa.is/media/throunarsamvinna/MFA-StrategyforIcelandsDevelopmentCooperation-2013-2016.pdf.

Other sources

GHD (2003), *23 Principles and Good Practice of Humanitarian Donorship*, Declaration made in Stockholm 16-17 June, Good Humanitarian Donorship initiative, www.ghdinitiative.org/ghd/gns/principles-good-practice-of-ghd/principles-good-practice-ghd.html.

OECD (2013a), "Special Review of Iceland", OECD, Paris, www.oecd.org/dac/dac-global-relations/Iceland%20Special%20Review.pdf.

OECD (2013b), *OECD Development Assistance Accession Report: Iceland 2012\1*, OECD, Paris.

OECD (2012), *Supporting Partners to Develop their Capacity, 12 Lessons from DAC Peer Reviews*, OECD, Paris, www.oecd.org/fr/cad/examens-pairs/Capacity12lessons.pdf.

Chapter 3: Allocating Iceland's official development assistance

Overall ODA volume

Indicator: The member makes every effort to meet ODA domestic and international targets

Iceland's official development assistance (ODA) comprises a small proportion of DAC members' total bilateral development co-operation funding. Yet Iceland stands out for its high share of ODA allocated to the world's poorest countries, much of which is spent in fragile states. In the wake of its severe economic and banking system crisis, Iceland has abandoned ambitions to dramatically scale-up its development co-operation, with ODA levels now expected to stabilise at around 0.26% of gross national income over the next five years. However, the government's new five-year budget framework for development co-operation can help to support a gradual and sustained increase of Iceland's ODA in line with its future economic growth, as well as to improve predictability for its partners.

Iceland's ODA volume and ODA/GNI ratio fluctuated in the wake of its financial crisis

Iceland joined the DAC in March 2013. It is the committee's smallest member in terms of aid volume, delivering USD 40 million in net ODA in 2015.

Iceland has a long-standing commitment to reach the UN's target of providing 0.7% of its gross national income (GNI) as ODA. This commitment is highlighted in Iceland's *Strategy for International Development Cooperation 2013-2016*, which spells out Iceland's ambition to join those countries in its region contributing more than 0.7% of GNI to ODA (MFA, 2013). Within the ODA envelope, the strategy set targets for bilateral spending at 40%, multilateral spending at 52% and allocations for civil society at 8%, with a minimum of 75% of allocations earmarked for priority sectors and cross-cutting issues, including a strong emphasis on gender responsive budgeting (see Chapter 5). While waiting for its new government to approve its development policy and action plan, Iceland's ODA allocations are governed through the government's five-year Statement of Fiscal Policy financial plan, as well as its 2017 budget law and accompanying explanatory note (MFA, 2016), where ODA/GNI targets are also stated.

In terms of generosity, Iceland ranks 17th out of 28 OECD development co-operation providers, having allocated 0.24% of its GNI for development co-operation in 2015. As Figure 3.1 shows, Iceland's aid volume and ODA/GNI ratio more than doubled between 2000 and 2008, when ODA rose to a high of 0.36%[1] of GNI. However, this ratio has since declined significantly, largely due to the financial crisis that plunged Iceland's economy into recession, causing its currency to collapse. The crisis, in turn, resulted in a decline in GNI and a very weak Icelandic *króna* against existing ODA commitments in foreign currency.

Chapter 3: Allocating Iceland's official development assistance

Figure 3.1 Trends in Iceland's net ODA, 1999-2015

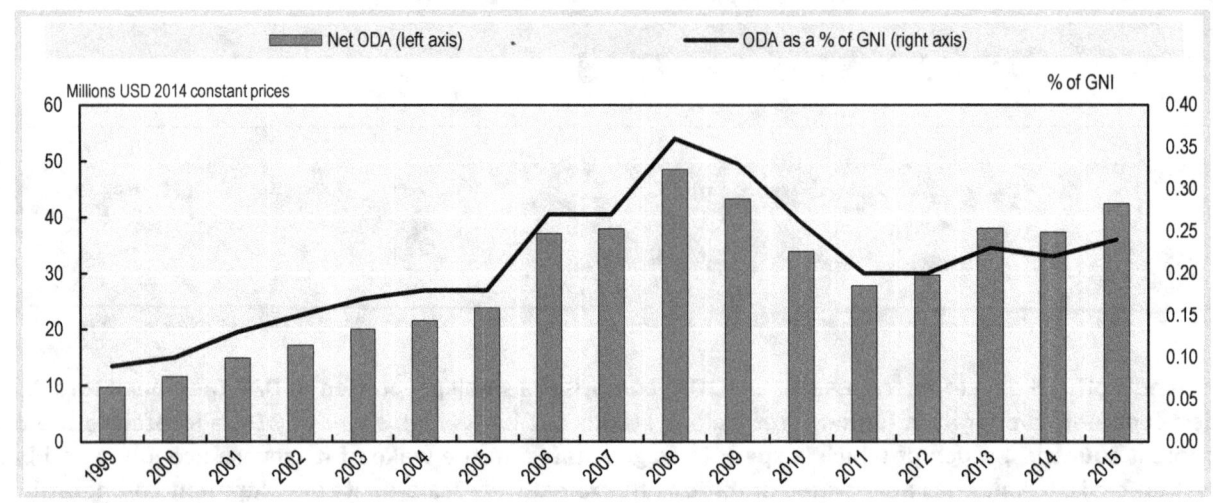

Source: Creditor Reporting System, accessed on 12 January 2017, https://stats.oecd.org/Index.aspx?DataSetCode=CRS1

The new budgetary framework should support a gradual and sustained ODA increase in line with Iceland's economic growth

Between 2008 and 2011, Iceland's ODA volume almost halved before restabilising at pre-crisis averages. During this period, Iceland exited three countries – Nicaragua, Namibia, and Sri Lanka – but remained engaged in Malawi, Mozambique, and Uganda.

Despite this setback, Iceland's *Strategy for Iceland's Development Co-operation 2013-2016* set out an ambitious timetable for its development assistance to reach the 0.7% target by 2019. In 2016, the Althingi adopted a revised plan for ODA levels to reach 0.26% of gross national income by 2018 and be maintained at this level until 2021. This timetable has not been amended in the 2013-2016 strategy, but is set out in Iceland's Statement of Fiscal Policy and Fiscal Strategy Plan 2017-21 (Althingi, 2016). While a more cautious approach in the wake of the financial crisis and ongoing policy challenges is understandable (OECD, 2015), these more modest increases do not reflect projections for robust growth (Statistics Iceland, 2016). Going forward, the government's new five-year budgetary framework, outlined further in Chapter 5, should help plan for a gradual and sustained increase in ODA in line with Iceland's economic growth.

Iceland is improving its reporting to the DAC

Iceland has improved the timeliness and comprehensiveness of its reporting of development co-operation data since it first joined the DAC in 2013. It is also working to improve the transparency of its ODA flows. However, given it does not yet provide indicative forward expenditures looking further than one year ahead, the latest progress report on the *Global Partnership for Effective Development Co-operation's 2016 Progress Report* calls for it to do more (OECD/UNDP, 2016). To deal with this unpredictability, multi-year indications of expenditures in country strategy papers include significant margins to reflect the uncertainties inherent in Iceland's annual state budget, as well as to take into account changing country circumstances. The new five-year budgetary framework is expected to help to improve predictability, allowing Iceland to report indicative resource allocations to partner countries in line with its commitment to the Busan partnership agreement to provide regular and timely information on forward expenditure plans.

Iceland provides all of its ODA as untied grants, excluding administrative costs and in-donor refugee costs. At present, data on other official flows and private flows at market terms from Iceland to developing countries are not available as Iceland does not have

Chapter 3: Allocating Iceland's official development assistance

specific private sector instruments. However, Iceland does raise a significant proportion of development funding through private grants (funds raised by non-government organisations and foundations), most notably through its national committees for UN Women and UNICEF. In the case of UNICEF, Icelandic private flows channelled through the national committee outstrip ODA flows (Chapter 1).

Bilateral ODA allocations
Indicator: Aid is allocated according to the statement of intent and international commitments

Iceland's bilateral allocations make up the vast bulk of its ODA, with spending increasingly concentrated on three least developed African countries in line with its geographic priorities. Iceland is commended for striving to increase the focus of its bilateral programme. Furthering these efforts by ensuring allocations are in line with the comparative advantages outlined in the *Strategy for Iceland's Development Cooperation 2013-2016*, and reducing the number of sectors in partner countries, would increase the cost-effectiveness of its bilateral programme.

Bilateral allocations are well concentrated on the poorest countries

Iceland's bilateral allocations make up the bulk of its ODA (more than 83% in 2014 and 78% in 2015), with spending concentrated[2] in three least developed countries: Malawi, Mozambique and Uganda.[3] This development assistance is delivered in three ways:

- through multi-bi (non-core) contributions to multilateral organisations (around one-third of Iceland's bilateral funding)
- as district-level programmes in partner countries
- as projects delivered by NGOs in response to calls for proposals.

The geographic allocation of Iceland's bilateral ODA is consistent with its commitment to focus on sub-Saharan Africa (Figure 3.2). As a result, the priority given by Iceland to least-developed countries remains high, representing more than 80% of bilateral allocable ODA (Annex A). This is double the average share of other DAC members in these countries.

Iceland's three priority bilateral partner countries are all fragile states (OECD, 2016). Iceland initially entered Malawi, Mozambique and Uganda because of its global comparative advantage in fisheries. Several evaluations and internal reviews found that this specific focus on fisheries had produced few sustainable results in all three countries.[4] As a result, Iceland has increasingly shifted its support to district-level social infrastructure and services – particularly in the health and education sectors (see Annex C). Iceland is already moving to better reflect this district-level work in the explanatory note accompanying its 2017 budget law in which health, education, water and sanitation are top-level priorities anchored in the Sustainable Development Goals (MFA, 2016). However, while Iceland's flexible and pragmatic approach to programming is commended, the sustainability of Iceland's efforts on social infrastructure and services in its partner countries has not yet been fully evaluated (see Chapter 5 on Iceland's plans to evaluate the Malawi programme in 2017, where sustainability remains a key concern).

Chapter 3: Allocating Iceland's official development assistance

Figure 3.2 Share of Iceland's gross bilateral ODA allocable by region, 2014-15

(by average, gross disbursements)

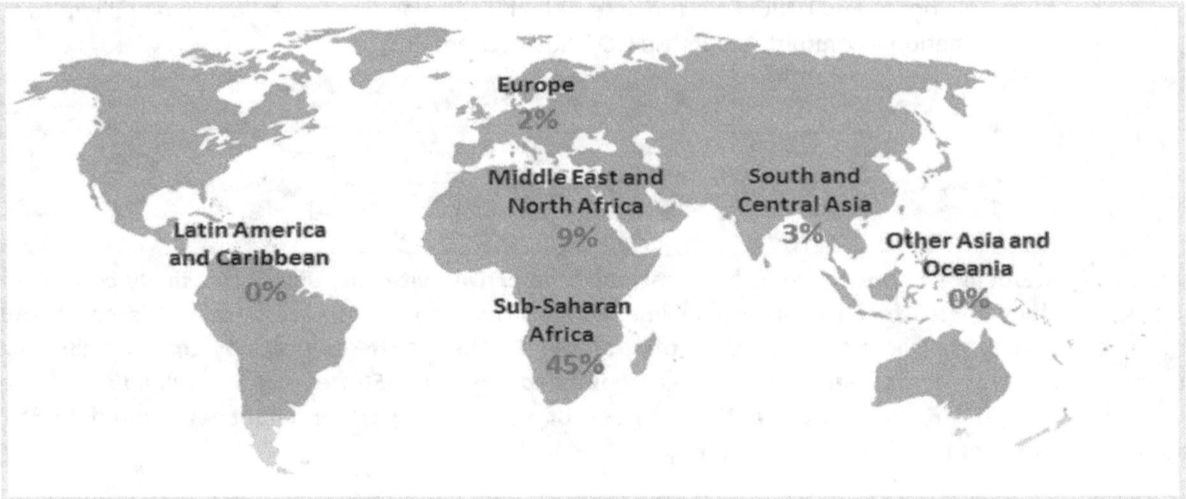

- Europe: 2%
- Middle East and North Africa: 9%
- South and Central Asia: 3%
- Latin America and Caribbean: 0%
- Other Asia and Oceania: 0%
- Sub-Saharan Africa: 45%

Note: 41% of bilateral ODA allocated was unspecified by region in 2014-15. This share is not represented on the map.

Source: OECD-DAC; www.oecd.org/dac/stats.

Iceland's bilateral aid concentrates on social infrastructure and sectors where it has established a global comparative advantage

The bulk of Iceland's bilateral aid (44%) went towards strengthening social infrastructure in education, health, water and sanitation, civil society and peace and security in 2014-15. In addition, allocations to projects in the energy sector amounted to 12 in 2014-15%, while 8% went to the fisheries sector. While the general move to social sectors in local communities in Malawi and Uganda demonstrates a flexible and pragmatic approach to programming, Iceland would do well to consider how to target its efforts where they can best offer value for money. For example, Iceland could deepen efforts to co-ordinate with other donors in specific sectors where it has an established global comparative advantage, as demonstrated through Iceland's allocations to a common fisheries fund for Mozambique led by Norway, which is increasing donor co-ordination and curbing aid fragmentation. Iceland is also pooling resources in its co-operation with key international partners on geothermal energy in East Africa (Chapter 1). These approaches are helping Iceland to increase its thematic focus, leverage additional resources and, ultimately, to improve the effectiveness of its development co-operation (Chapter 5).

An increasing proportion of Iceland's bilateral ODA is also being spent on refugee costs within Iceland (around 12% of gross disbursements in 2015, up from 8% in 2014 and 1% in 2013). To date, thanks to Iceland's strengthening economy, this increase has been absorbed in the programme without affecting aid commitments overseas. Short-term increases in these costs are expected to be covered by additional allocations reserved for support to refugees and asylum seekers in 2015-2016 (Government of Iceland, 2015).

Multilateral ODA channel
Indicator: The member uses the multilateral aid channels effectively

Iceland is an appreciated and engaged partner in the multilateral system, championing start-up initiatives and supporting key reforms. To increase the effectiveness of its limited resources, Iceland is increasing its engagement with its preferred multilateral partners, backed up by increasing funding to and through these organisations. It is also working to improve the predictability of its funding through framework agreements.

Increased multilateral ODA reflects Iceland's increased focus on multilateral engagement

Iceland's share of multilateral aid was 22 % in 2015, with core contributions concentrated on the World Bank, UNICEF and UN Women. However, when core contributions are combined with non-core contributions (bilateral allocations through multilateral channels), contributions to and through multilateral organisations have amounted to more than half of Iceland's total gross ODA in recent years (Figure 3.3). Indeed, total funding to and through multilateral channels increased by 19% in 2015 due in part to Iceland's delayed replenishment of the World Bank's International Development Association funding and other multilateral organisations (Government of Iceland, 2016). Iceland is now working to improve the predictability and flexibility of its multilateral allocations. As Figure 3.3 shows, while non-core funding has fallen slightly since 2013, Iceland has increased core funding to key multilateral partners in recent years, recording one of the largest increases of 47% from 2014 to 2015. This trend is expected to continue (Government of Iceland, 2016).

In general, Iceland allocates its multilateral aid in line with its strategy and good practice principles for this channel, with allocations concentrated on its core priorities: gender, sustainable fisheries and energy. However, the extent to which support to the UNU's activities in Iceland aligns with Iceland's objective to eradicate poverty and geographical focus of its programmes is under scrutiny (Chapter 2). Its role as a contributor to UNICEF and UN Women is highly appreciated, particularly as Iceland moves to framework agreements with these organisations in an effort to make its allocations more predictable and effective through lighter earmarking and increasing core contributions. Iceland also channels a significant part of its bilateral ODA to multilateral organisations through non-core contributions in its priority countries, representing an additional one-third of its bilateral ODA. Overall feedback from multilateral organisations suggests that Iceland is an active stakeholder, engaged in the management of its priority organisations. It champions start-up initiatives and is an advocate of key reforms, for example on further integrating cross-cutting issues such as environmental sustainability and gender equality in programming (Chapter 1).

Chapter 3: Allocating Iceland's official development assistance

Figure 3.3 Iceland's official development assistance to multilateral organisations, 2011-15

(a) Gross disbursements, constant 2014 thousand USD

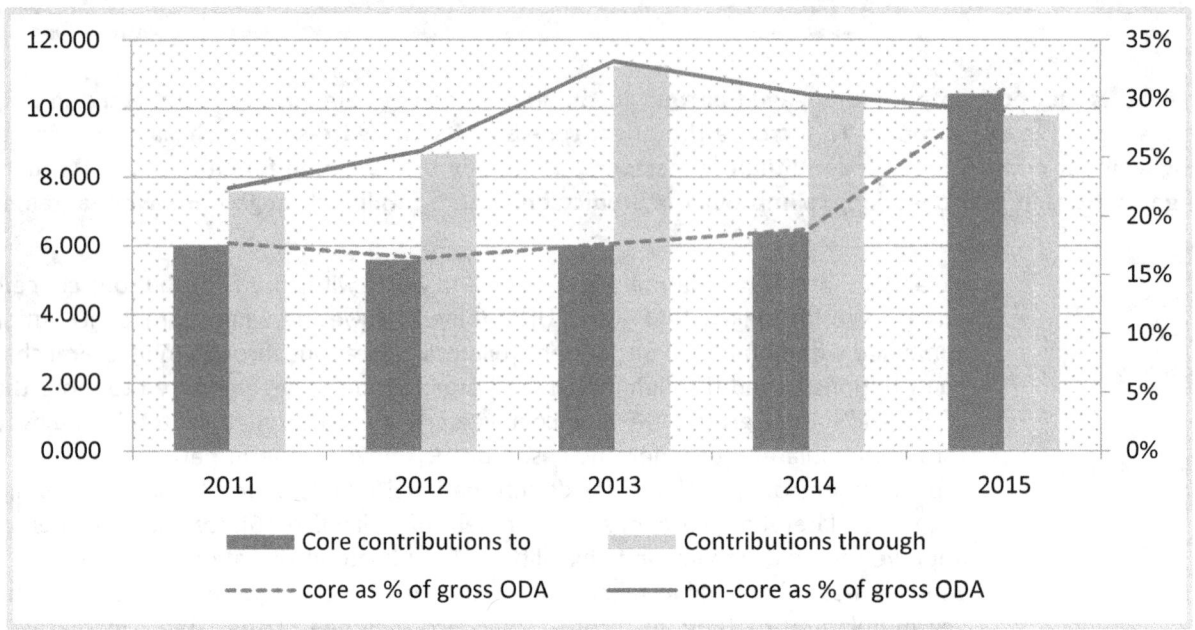

Source: DAC tables, accessed on 6 January 2017, https://stats.oecd.org/Index.aspx?ataSetCode=CRS1.

(b) Iceland's total use of the multilateral system, 2015

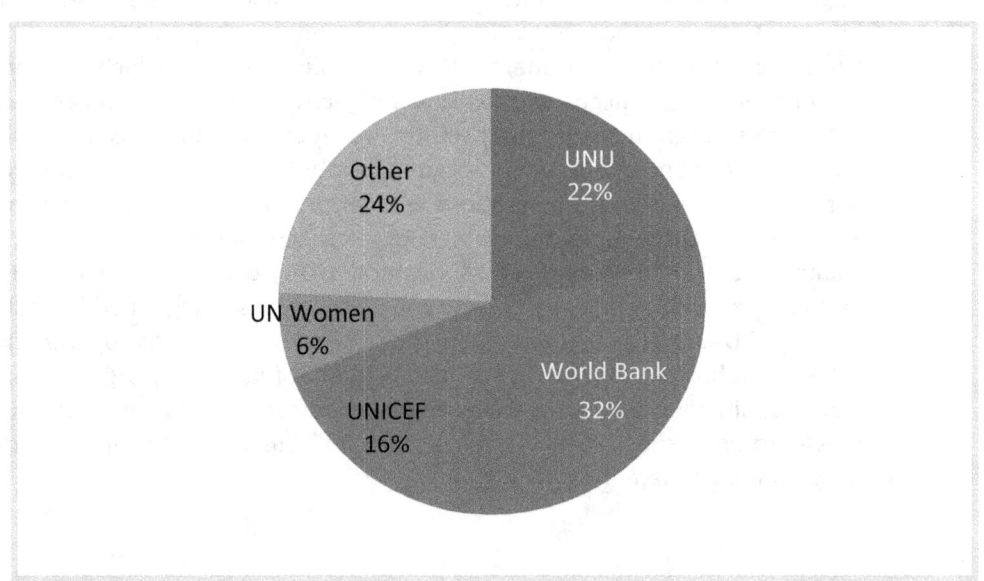

Source: Creditor Reporting System, "Members' total use of the multilateral system", accessed on 6 January 2017, https://stats.oecd.org/Index.aspx?DataSetCode=CRS1.

Chapter 3: Allocating Iceland's official development assistance

Notes

1. As Iceland notes in its memorandum (Government of Iceland, 2016), the banking system crash of 2008 heavily affected the country's GNI, which makes the ODA proportion difficult to identify. Where Iceland's official statistics differ from OECD statistics we have deferred to OECD statistics.

2. While it is recognised good practice for significant-sized DAC members to concentrate their bilateral ODA on an optimum number of partner countries, Iceland is not considered a significant donor (i.e. among the top 10 donors) in any of its partner countries. This guidance must, therefore be seen in the context of Iceland's small programme.

3. The DAC's Special Review of Iceland (OECD, 2013a) noted that allocations to its priority countries of Uganda, Malawi and Mozambique accounted for 38% of its bilateral aid between 2010 and 2011; this had risen to 44% in 2016 (Government of Iceland, 2016).

4. For example, see the mid-term review of Iceland's assistance to the fisheries sector of Mozambique (Government of Iceland, 2012) or the report on the status of fisheries and fishing communities in Uganda's Buikwe District (Government of Iceland, 2013).

Chapter 3: Allocating Iceland's official development assistance

Bibliography

Government sources

Althingi (2015), *Amendment to Act No 121/2008 (Act 122/2015),* entered into force January 2016, Reykjavik.

Althingi (2012), *Amendment to Act No 121/2008 (Act 161/2012),* enacted January 2013, Reykjavik.

Althingi (2008), *Act on Iceland's International Development Co-operation (Act 121/2008)*, Reykjavik, www.mfa.is/media/MFA_pdf/Act-on-Icelands-International-Development-Cooperation.pdf.

Government of Iceland (2015), "Two billion ISK reserved for support to refugees and asylum seekers", Prime Minister's Office press release, 20 September, https://eng.forsaetisraduneyti.is/news-and-articles/nr/8594.

Government of Iceland (2011), *A Parliamentary Resolution on a Strategy for Iceland's International Development Co-operation 2011-2014.* Adopted by the Althingi 10 June 2011.

ICEIDA (2013), *Geothermal Exploration Project, NDF 2013-2017*, Icelandic International Development Agency, Reykjavik, www.iceida.is/iceida-projects/current-projects/nr/1488.

ICEIDA (2012), *Guiding Principles for Addressing Environmental Issues*, Icelandic International Development Agency, Reykjavik, www.iceida.is/media/pdf/Guiding-Principles-for-Environmental-Issues.pdf.

MFA (2016), Explanatory note on development co-operation for Iceland's budget bill, adopted on 22 December 2016 (now the 2017 budget law). Ministry for Foreign Affairs, Reykjavik.

MFA (2013), *Strategy for Iceland's International Development Cooperation (2013-2016)*, (Icelandic only, highlights available in English), Ministry for Foreign Affairs, Reykjavik, www.mfa.is/media/throunarsamvinna/MFA-StrategyforIcelandsDevelopmentCooperation-2013-2016.pdf.

Statistics Iceland (2016), *"Economy expected to grow by 4.8% during 2016 and 4.4% in 2017"*, press release from the National Statistics Institute of Iceland, available at www.statice.is/publications/news-archive/economic-forecast/economic-forecast-winter-2016.

Other sources

GHD (2003), *23 Principles and Good Practice of Humanitarian Donorship,* Stockholm 16-17 June www.ghdinitiative.org/ghd/gns/principles-good-practice-of-ghd/principles-good-practice-ghd.html.

OECD (2015), OECD Economic Surveys: Iceland 2015, OECD Publishing, http://dx.doi.org/10.1787/eco_surveys-isl-2015-en.

OECD (2013a), "Special Review of Iceland", OECD, Paris, www.oecd.org/dac/dac-global-relations/Iceland%20Special%20Review.pdf.

OECD (2013b), *OECD Development Assistance Accession Report: Iceland 2012\1*, OECD, Paris.

OECD (2012), *Supporting Partners to Develop their Capacity, 12 Lessons from DAC Peer Reviews*, OECD, Paris. www.oecd.org/fr/cad/examens-pairs/Capacity12lessons.pdf

Chapter 4: Managing Iceland's development co-operation

Institutional system

Indicator: The institutional structure is conducive to consistent, quality development co-operation

Iceland is bedding down the integration of its bilateral development agency within the Ministry for Foreign Affairs – a move which is strengthening its institutional framework and operational capacity for development co-operation. The merger has safeguarded country-level bilateral structures, enabling Iceland to honour its commitments to partner countries. The new arrangements, including a single advisory body on development co-operation, should be kept under review to ensure Iceland can continue to implement its aid effectively.

Iceland has strengthened its institutional framework to deliver quality development co-operation

In 2016, Iceland integrated its bilateral development agency, ICEIDA, within the Ministry for Foreign Affairs, which had been overseeing all of Iceland's multilateral development co-operation, including the bilateral programmes implemented by international organisations and non-government organisations. This decision came about following two reviews commissioned by the Icelandic Government, which found that the development co-operation system – whereby two organisations were managing ODA – was stifling competence, flexibility and co-ordination (OECD, 2013; Gudmundsson, 2014). This system was also contributing to high transaction and overhead costs. These shortcomings were exacerbated by budget cuts that followed Iceland's economic crisis (Chapter 3), a more concentrated aid programme (Chapter 2), and ICEIDA's shift towards district-level programming in partner countries (Chapter 5).

The integration is a two-step process: first, all ICEIDA functions were brought under the Ministry for Foreign Affairs, which now manages around 88% of Iceland's ODA. Within the ministry, the Directorate of International Development Cooperation is now responsible for Iceland's development co-operation policy formulation, planning, administration, evaluation and co-ordination (Annex B). The Director General oversees this work and is also Iceland's Ambassador for the three countries where ICEIDA had missions.[1] Second, the ministry is now building internal consensus for additional reforms to continue integrating the two institutional cultures.

The decision to bring development co-operation under a single ministry has improved the co-ordination and alignment of Iceland's foreign and development co-operation policies. The merger has enabled more effective development co-operation, simplified administrative procedures and reduced the number of actors engaged in consultations. Importantly, the ministry settled for a new organisational structure that breaks down silos and that builds synergies across channels of delivery and approaches. For example, the new organisational set-up will include an evaluation unit to assess the most important development co-operation activities,[2] while monitoring is integrated across the directorate (Chapter 6). It is also noteworthy that the merger safeguarded Iceland's country-level commitments, but field missions now receive directions from only one institution. This is particularly important in fragile contexts (e.g. Malawi, Mozambique, and Uganda), where situations can quickly deteriorate and decision making needs to be swift.

Chapter 4: Managing Iceland's development co-operation

However, as the merger only took effect on 1 January 2016, Iceland will need to keep its new institutional arrangements under review and adapt them, as necessary, so that it can continue implementing its programme effectively. In particular, the Ministry for Foreign Affairs will need to co-ordinate with other ministries to ensure that the recent increase of in-donor refugee costs remains additional to its ODA commitments overseas (Chapter 3).

Structures exist for whole-of-government co-ordination, but they could exert more influence

Iceland's integrated setup makes co-ordination relatively easy. Within the ministry, the Permanent Secretary of State meets on a weekly basis with the five Directors-General and the Chief of Protocol to discuss issues regarding the ministry. These meetings provide an opportunity for the development co-operation Director General to inform others on activities related to development co-operation (Figure B.1, Annex B). This structure allows Iceland's development co-operation to be more integrated with foreign policy.

Compared to other DAC members, Iceland has a relatively small number of government actors in the field of development co-operation. Other than the Ministry for Foreign Affairs, there are eight ministries that work, directly or indirectly, on development-related issues. Co-ordination with these ministries happens through:

- Formal mechanisms (i.e. joint strategies, memoranda of understanding), in which the Ministry for Foreign Affairs co-ordinates and collaborates with one or various ministries on development co-operation. For example, Iceland's regional programme on geothermal energy in the East African Rift Valley (Chapter 5) draws on expertise from the Ministry of Environment and Natural Resources.

- Inter-ministerial committees that can be created ad hoc to discuss and co-ordinate an issue and which may lead to an inter-ministerial mechanism, as described above. For example, an ad hoc committee gathered in 2015 in the Prime Minister's Office and the ministries of foreign affairs, interior and welfare to manage the arrival of asylum seekers.

The recent refugee crisis has created new imperatives for whole-of-government co-ordination and Iceland recognises more generally the need for more systematic policy co-ordination. Iceland could continue making good use of these structures to ensure strategic co-ordination and to leverage relevant expertise on development-related matters. Furthermore, Iceland could also use these co-ordination mechanisms to raise awareness of how various ministries can contribute to the national development co-operation system, and to build capacity across government in development co-operation. The Ministry for Foreign Affairs will also need to review its co-ordination with the Ministry of Finance on Iceland's contributions to the recently-created Asian Infrastructure Investment Bank.

In its partner countries, Iceland has an opportunity to enhance cross-government planning tools and structures

Iceland's development co-operation setup promotes an integrated response in its three partner countries. Its embassies in these countries have the same mandate and budget as before the merger but now receive only one direction from headquarters. The embassies' input to the Ministry for Foreign Affairs now occurs through the Director General of the Directorate of International Development Cooperation, who is also the Ambassador to these countries. This structure is already improving co-ordination and cutting transaction costs.

At the same time, the incorporation of ICEIDA's field missions into the ministry's foreign service affords an opportunity to expand these missions' mandate beyond development co-operation. Foreign missions could work on other development-related issues such as

Chapter 4: Managing Iceland's development co-operation

trade, environment and energy.[3] Doing so would help the ministry better understand the impact of Iceland's policies in developing countries and could be another way to engage the line ministries in development-related activities.

Iceland's development co-operation structure benefits from a stronger advisory system

The Icelandic development co-operation system has also reformed its advisory structures (Figure 4.1). Until 2015, Iceland had two advisory bodies, the Development Cooperation Committee and the Council on International Development Cooperation. According to the two reviews mentioned above, these bodies duplicated work because of their overlapping composition and weak relations with parliament (OECD, 2013; Gudmundsson, 2014). This hampered their ability to discuss and lead on development co-operation. The reviews also noted that both bodies could integrate their resources to provide better advice on Iceland's development co-operation.

In 2016, a Committee on International Development Cooperation replaced the former bodies (Figure 4.1), and has a new composition and stronger mandate. The committee is now Iceland's only forum for strategic dialogue and advises both the minister and the Ministry for Foreign Affairs on policy formulation and implementation of Iceland's development co-operation. The committee meets at least twice a year with the Minister for Foreign Affairs and includes Icelandic civil society organisations, academia and social partners, as well as parliamentarians. This new approach is already improving awareness and understanding of development co-operation in Iceland's parliament. Given Iceland's small size, it can be commended for streamlining its advisory institutions. However, as this reform is recent, Iceland will need to monitor – and adapt if necessary – the new setup so that relevant stakeholders can continue adding value to the system.

Figure 4.1 Iceland's new development co-operation system

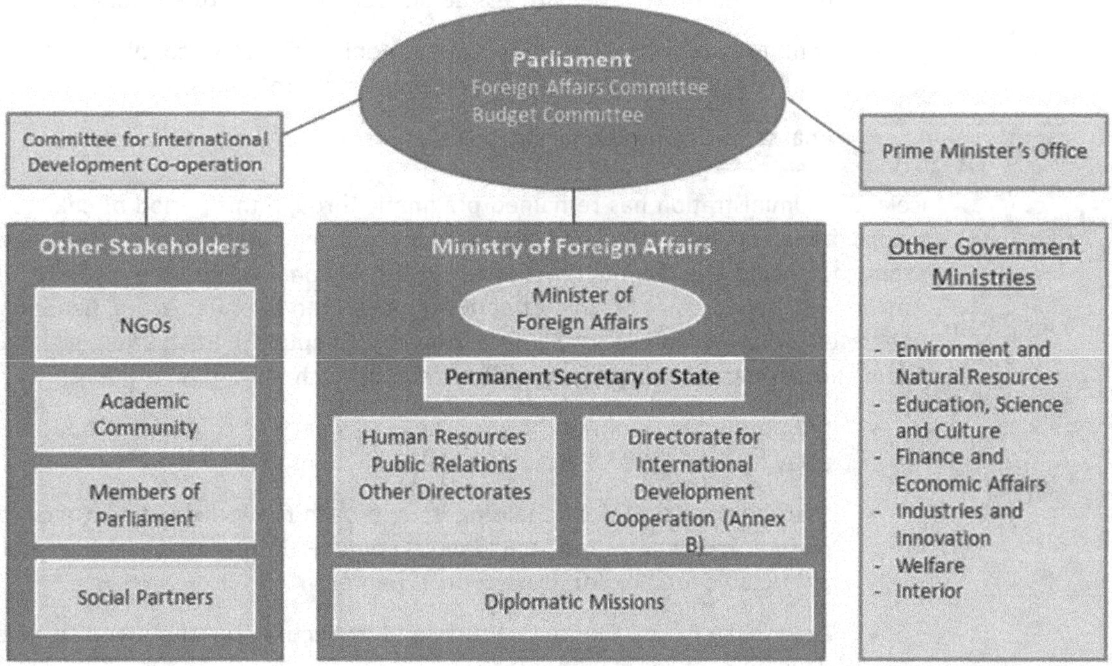

Source: Author's compilation.

Chapter 4: Managing Iceland's development co-operation

Adaptation to change
Indicator: The system is able to reform and innovate to meet evolving needs

Iceland's commitments to its implementing partners were central priorities during and after the integration of its former development agency with the Ministry for Foreign Affairs. While it is too early to assess the full impact of the merger on Iceland's ability to carry out effective development co-operation, efficiency gains are already observable.

The Icelandic system has adapted well to change but further management reforms are required

The merger between the Ministry for Foreign Affairs and Iceland's former bilateral development co-operation agency, ICEIDA, has demonstrated that Iceland is able to adapt to changing circumstances. The ministry aimed to keep the best elements of the previous two development co-operation institutions by retaining those methods and approaches in the short-term that were working well, while promoting an inclusive change management process in the medium term. For example, the use of targets to track the implementation of the Busan principles on effective development co-operation is still in place (OECD, 2011).

The merger was announced in December 2015 and took effect shortly afterwards – in January 2016. This created anxiety and uncertainty for former ICEIDA staff. To smooth the transition, Iceland contracted a consultant specialised in change management to help build a joint vision for the new development co-operation team. However, Iceland will need to pay heed to a number of issues to ensure that the merger can be sustained in the future. In particular, it will need to.

- take stock of how the merger process was managed and reflect on how the lessons learnt from this process could feed into any future reforms
- continue to reflect on how to harmonise different conditions of service for staff (e.g. salary scales, policy for training staff, rotations)
- finalise its organisational structure and corresponding unit functions.

Iceland's pragmatic and flexible approach provides a solid basis for adapting to new circumstances

Iceland's administration has remained pragmatic through this period of change, providing a solid basis for innovation and adaptation to change. To promote good practice, for example, Iceland has recently implemented the regional geothermal project for the East African Rift Valley using a cost-effective model that operates from headquarters and integrates triangular and South-South exchanges (Chapter 5). In addition, Iceland has been testing novel operational approaches (for Iceland), such as:

- promoting programmatic approaches in its partner countries (Chapter 5), moving away from traditional project-based implementation
- sharpening and professionalising its approach to working in partnership with key non-governmental and multilateral organisations, emphasising stability and predictable funding for its partners (Chapter 5)
- expanding its evaluation culture and reflecting on the need to manage for development results (Chapter 6).

Furthermore, Iceland's flexible approach – including in fragile settings – is perceived as a comparative advantage by partner countries, NGOs and multilateral organisations.[4]

Chapter 4: Managing Iceland's development co-operation

Human resources

Indicator: The member manages its human resources effectively to respond to field imperatives

In response to a drop in official development assistance, Iceland reduced the number of its development co-operation staff. These numbers have now stabilised but Iceland needs to be aware of the risk of diluting development expertise in its new integrated foreign affairs system. Improving incentives for development as a career path, retaining and developing expertise through careful planning of rotations and a focus on training needs for development professionals and diplomats across the ministry can all reduce this risk and enhance the effectiveness of Iceland's development co-operation.

Iceland has reduced staffing levels as a result of its economic crisis

Iceland's acute economic crisis led to a reduction in the numbers of professional staff working on development co-operation from over 50 in 2012-3 to 46 in 2016 (Table 4.1).

Table 4.1 Number of staff (full-time equivalent), 2012-16

	Dec 2012	Dec 2013	Dec 2015	Dec 2016
Total staff in Reykjavik				
• ICEIDA staff	12	10	9	
• MFA staff	9	9	11	21
Posted staff at missions	5	7	6	6
Locally engaged staff at missions	25.5	28	19	19
TOTAL STAFF	51.5	54	45	46

Source: Communications with the Ministry for Foreign Affairs of Iceland

A positive feature of Iceland's development co-operation is its high proportion of field staff. In fact, staff levels in foreign missions have represented the majority of all staff since 2012. Most field staff are locally-employed and manage programmes and represent Iceland in technical and policy dialogue with district authorities. In conflict-affected areas, Iceland also seconds technical staff (and other staff managed by the Icelandic Crisis Response Unit) through international organisations such as the North Atlantic Treaty Organisation, Organisation for Security and Co-operation in Europe and United Nations missions. This allows Iceland to support crisis management processes effectively despite a limited budget.

Iceland faces a number of obstacles to managing human resources effectively

The staff working in the former bilateral development co-operation agency ICEIDA have years of field experience and expertise in areas where Iceland believes it has a comparative advantage, while ministry diplomats are knowledgeable about multilateral development co-operation and trade. This combined expertise will help Iceland deliver more effective aid and support the implementation of the Sustainable Development Goals.

However, Iceland faces a number of human resource challenges. For example, Iceland is aware of the skills that need filling through recruitment or training (e.g. humanitarian assistance, global public goods or results management). At the same time, with only three and a half human resource staff positions for the whole Ministry for Foreign Affairs, capacity limitations must also be taken into account.

When ICEIDA existed, training was planned systematically, whereas in the ministry, diplomats received limited development-related training. Nevertheless, Iceland now plans to systematically provide training in results-based management and evaluation for development staff, and will continue to provide security training before deployment in a crisis context. Iceland will need to keep its approach for training and staff development under review in the future, especially to ensure that diplomats receive development-related training. Failure to train new Ministry recruits would risk diluting development co-operation expertise, particularly given the ministry's rotation system (whereby staff are posted to field missions and change positions in headquarters that require no development expertise).

Notes

1. These countries are Malawi, Mozambique and Uganda. After the merger, ICEIDA's partner country offices were integrated into the Ministry for Foreign Affairs' network of foreign missions.

2. Before the merger, evaluation functions were carried out by ICEIDA.

3. Iceland's three priority bilateral countries – Malawi, Mozambique and Uganda – have all prioritised energy in their development plans and all have some geothermal energy potential.

4. Within conflict contexts, however, such as in Afghanistan or the Middle East, Iceland's development co-operation is too limited to be adjusted if the context deteriorates.

Chapter 4: Managing Iceland's development co-operation

Bibliography

Government sources

Althingi (2015), *Commentary on Amendments to Act no. 121/2008*, Althingi, Reykjavik.

Althingi (2008), *Act on Iceland's International Development Cooperation (Act No. 121/2008)*, Althingi, Reykjavik, www.mfa.is/media/MFA_pdf/Act-on-Icelands-International-Development-Cooperation.pdf.

Government of Iceland (2016), "OECD DAC peer review of Iceland: memorandum", Government of Iceland, Reykjavik.

MFA (2013), *Strategy for Iceland's International Development Cooperation (2013-2016)*, Ministry for Foreign Affairs, Reykjavik, www.mfa.is/media/throunarsamvinna/MFA-StrategyforIcelandsDevelopmentCooperation-2013-2016.pdf.

Other sources

Gudmundsson, T. (2014), "Review of Iceland's organisational structure for development co-operation, humanitarian assistance and peacebuilding", manuscript.

OECD (2013), "Special Review of Iceland", OECD, Paris, www.oecd.org/dac/dac-global-relations/Iceland%20Special%20Review.pdf.

OECD (2011), "Busan Partnership for Effective Development Co-operation", Fourth High Level Forum on Aid Effectiveness, Busan, Republic of Korea, 29 November-1 December 2011, OECD, Paris, www.oecd.org/dac/effectiveness/49650173.pdf.

Chapter 5: Iceland's development co-operation delivery and partnerships

Budgeting and programming processes

Indicator: These processes support quality aid as defined in Busan

Iceland takes its commitment to the Busan principles for effective development very seriously. This is reflected in its development co-operation strategy and tight, effective operations on the ground. In particular, Iceland makes good use of district-level systems, is well aligned with national and district development plans, co-ordinates meaningfully with other donors, unties all of its aid and makes limited use of conditionality. In addition, Iceland is improving the predictability of its programming and budgeting processes, which are helping it to respond and adjust to the needs of its partners.

Iceland's rolling five-year budgetary framework will improve predictability and flexibility

Iceland's strategy for development co-operation (2013-16) provides an overarching framework for how it should provide quality aid, as defined in Busan (OECD, 2011a). Importantly, the strategy includes an indicative budget for Iceland's bilateral grants and requires that multi-year country and regional strategy papers also refer to overall and annual minimum and maximum expenditures. The budget allocated to bilateral operations, reflected in country strategy papers, is negotiated with local stakeholders on the basis of district development plans and is aligned with local budgeting systems (e.g. accounting tools, monitoring indicators). In this way, Iceland honours its Busan commitments, while introducing flexibility and scalability into its operations, trying to take account of the fluctuations in its annual budgetary process.

Discussions in Reykjavik on planning for Iceland's new development co-operation policy and action plan an intention to continue with previous practice of using targets in humanitarian assistance and core contributions to multilateral organisations. The rationale for introducing these targets is to avoid large deviations from stated priorities; however, Iceland will need to be flexible in implementing these targets so it can continue responding to its partners with assistance when needed.

In addition, Iceland has reformed its entire public financing legislation to introduce rolling five-year budgetary frameworks (vs. the current three-year cycles).[1] This reform also applies to Iceland's aid and will ensure more predictability for its partners (see chapters 2 and 3). While this reform brings Iceland's development co-operation budget planning into line with overall governmental budget processes, Iceland will still need to ensure coherence between its commitment to increase aid levels over time and the funds allocated for this purpose. Moreover, as the aid budget is approved annually, the Ministry for Foreign Affairs may still not receive the budget necessary to implement its policy commitments, which could diminish future predictability.

Chapter 5: Iceland's development co-operation delivery and partnerships

Programmes are aligned with district priorities and build capacity in partner countries

Iceland's bilateral development co-operation concentrates on building the capacity of local stakeholders to provide essential social services (health, water and sanitation, education) at district level in Malawi and Uganda. Programming is well-aligned with partner country and district priorities, as well as partner planning and budgeting cycles at district level, which is good practice. Country strategy papers are prepared in consultation with national governments, district councils, traditional authorities and other domestic stakeholders, including other donors that work at national and district level. These papers have taken a programmatic approach since 2012, which exemplify how Iceland is shifting from a project mentality to one of working through programmes and partnerships to build capacity and achieve results. This approach is helping to transfer responsibilities to Iceland's district-level partners and is fostering local ownership, increasing the effectiveness of its programme.

Iceland's bilateral delivery model also benefits from flexible budgetary procedures (Box 5.1). The Ministry for Foreign Affairs has a single budget line for development co-operation, which is enhancing transparency and promoting flexibility internally. Once the ministry receives the annual aid envelope, funds for bilateral development co-operation (except for the regional programme on geothermal energy)[2] are transferred to Iceland's field missions. Iceland's missions have some degree of flexibility to react to changing local circumstances, which is particularly important given that Iceland operates in fragile contexts.

Box 5.1 Example of Iceland's scenario planning

When drafting country papers, Iceland's field missions – together with the Ministry for Foreign Affairs – introduce three scenarios to guide bilateral co-operation over a given period of time. These scenarios are linked with minimum and maximum financial commitments from Iceland and introduce an element of flexibility and scalability in Iceland's programming at country level.

In practice, Iceland usually uses the minimum scenario, which also acts as a "floor" below which its aid does not fall. Nevertheless, even within this scenario Iceland is able to adapt as the context changes. Missions can deviate from stated objectives to respond to local changes by up to 10% of the total amount received. For example, Iceland was able to support Malawi in such a manner after the drought and floods of 2012-13 and 2015 respectively by re-directing funds to NGOs and the World Food Programme (Annex C). Beyond the 10% threshold, the ministry needs to approve and assess any field request.

Source: Government of Iceland (2016), "OECD DAC peer review of Iceland: Memorandum"; interviews in Reykjavik (September 2016).

Iceland is making good progress in using district-level systems

Iceland has signed up to the Paris Declaration, Accra Agenda of Action and Busan Outcome Document and adheres to the principles which underpin the Global Partnership for Effective Development Co-operation (OECD, 2011a). Iceland monitors progress on a number of these principles and has been improving its performance over time. Moreover, Iceland performs better than the DAC average on most of the indicators that it monitors and for which DAC data are available (Table 5.1).

Chapter 5: Iceland's development co-operation delivery and partnerships

Table 5.1 Iceland's progress against selected aid effectiveness targets, 2009-2015

Indicators	Baseline 2009	Targets in 2014	Progress in 2015	DAC Average
% ODA on national budget of partner country	21%	85%	75%	49%
% ODA that is technical assistance and aligned to partner country strategies	N/A	70%	75%	85%
%ODA using partner country's public financial management systems	2%	70%	75%	52%
% Iceland's procurement using the national procurement systems of the partner countries	32%	70%	75%	43%
Number of parallel Project Implementation Units	54	0	2	N/A

Note: The DAC average is unweighted and does not include data for Greece and Poland.

Source: Government of Iceland (2016), "OECD DAC peer review of Iceland: Memorandum"; compiled by authors using the Global Partnership for Effective Development Co-operation database, http://effectivecooperation.org/monitoring-country-progress/explore-monitoring-data/.

Iceland's activities place a strong focus on using district-level systems, transferring knowledge and building the capacity of counterparts. In its bilateral partner countries, Iceland uses district estimates for the planning process, and district systems for financial management (e.g. manual accounting systems) and procurement. Funds are directly disbursed to district councils using their public budgetary frameworks, and district indicators are used for monitoring outputs and outcomes (financial and programmatic).

In Malawi's Mangochi District, for example, Iceland started using district-level systems after years of building district capacities, researching district financial processes and procedures, and assessing the district's ability to absorb the funds and build a reporting module, using existing data indicators. As a result, Iceland now uses the district's financial management information system to handle and track disbursed funds. In addition, Iceland uses local procurement systems. In cases where inefficiencies emerge, Iceland provides hands-on support to its partners to build capacity and improve shortcomings – a laudable approach. Following the success of this approach, Iceland is currently transferring lessons to its mission in Uganda and to other donors working in Mangochi.

Iceland analyses risks and applies performance-based conditions to mitigate risks

To analyse risk and opportunities, Iceland relies on: (1) preparatory work before launching field-work; (2) several years of experience in the field; and (3) knowledge gathered from other donors. Through these activities, Iceland is able to build a knowledge base that then helps it to assess fiduciary, political economy and macroeconomic risks and identify opportunities. This information feeds into the programming process.

For example, Iceland's participation in the Heads of Cooperation Group in Malawi ensured it was informed on the so-called "Cashgate" corruption scandal, which led to the introduction of appropriate risk mitigation tools to prevent corruption at district level. In Malawi, Iceland's disbursements are now conditional on a positive assessment by its field missions of the district's quarterly report of expenditures and progress. This approach is combined with a monthly visit by Iceland's field staff to the district councils. Through these visits, Icelandic staff can identify and fill any capacity gaps that may hinder appropriate reporting.

Chapter 5: Iceland's development co-operation delivery and partnerships

Icelandic aid is 100% untied

Iceland is fully committed to keeping its aid untied. Since 2012, 100% of its aid has been untied (excluding administrative and in-donor refugee costs). This is in line with the international commitments that Iceland made in Accra and Busan (OECD, 2011a). As a result, Iceland's share of untied aid is above the DAC average of 89.6% (latest data from 2013).

Iceland applies few conditions

Iceland has no policy on conditionality and only applies performance-based conditions to its district activities. When conditions are used, they are agreed mutually and are based on clear performance results and reporting requirements. Iceland's use of conditionality is therefore aimed at improving development outcomes and devised as a risk mitigation tool.

Partnerships

Indicator: The member makes appropriate use of co-ordination arrangements, promotes strategic partnerships to develop synergies, and enhances mutual accountability

Iceland takes a pragmatic approach to co-ordination and partnership. In its bilateral operations, it applies the principle of division of labour and forges partnerships with district authorities, with a strong focus on capacity building. However, partnerships with other donors and with non-governmental organisations could be enhanced to ensure that Iceland can deliver quality aid.

Iceland makes good use of co-ordination mechanisms, especially with Nordic donors

Iceland is aware that co-ordination with other donors can maximise the impact of its limited resources. This is why Iceland is engaged in policy dialogue and co-ordination at country level, working closely with and learning from other donors when it can, as well as contributing to donors' learning. Iceland also supports joint initiatives that contribute to donor harmonisation and reduce the burden of fragmented aid on partners, while applying the division of labour principle. This co-operation mainly takes place with other Nordic donors and can be considered good practice.

In Mozambique, Iceland and Norway operate a common fisheries fund; in Uganda Iceland worked with Norway and Denmark to promote gender-responsive climate change mitigation and adaptation, and with Belgium on an entrepreneurship training programme. Furthermore, Iceland co-operates with the Nordic Development Fund to implement its regional geothermal project in the East African Rift Valley and El Salvador. It also co-operates with the Nordic nations to channel messages to key multilateral organisations working in its partner countries (e.g. UN Women, the World Bank or UNICEF). This high level of co-ordination is to be commended because it helps Iceland to spread risks and build synergies with other donors, and ensures that Iceland works in areas where it adds value.

Iceland is a strong advocate of greater donor co-ordination and improved alignment with partner countries. Where donor co-ordination bodies do not exist, Iceland liaises with donors informally to exchange relevant information and lessons learned. However, as discussed in Reykjavik, Iceland could make greater use of existing relationships at national level in its key partner countries to continue assessing where and how it can add most

Chapter 5: Iceland's development co-operation delivery and partnerships

value in its district-level work and to ensure the sustainability of its investments. For example, Iceland could assess how its pilot project to gather together health sector donors operating in Malawi has improved local co-ordination and helped Malawi achieve better development results in this sector.

Iceland emphasises mutual accountability in its partner countries

Iceland's main instruments for mutual accountability are the district-level sectoral strategies (education, health, water and sanitation) that are negotiated and discussed with national ministries and district councils. District councils monitor and report on programme implementation quarterly, while joint commissions discuss implementation challenges that can potentially lead to the suspension of disbursements. Iceland relies on district-level information and planning, and should be commended for its approach to working with local authorities.

However, Iceland only monitors and discusses the outputs and outcomes of its programmes – it is not yet monitoring or evaluating the results of its interventions. Iceland could therefore make greater use of joint results monitoring activities to learn more about the kind of development results it is having, which in turn would strengthen mutual accountability.

Iceland has strong partnerships with a range of actors

Iceland is engaged in numerous strategic partnerships to increase the impact of its development co-operation. Engaging with many partners helps Iceland leverage its technical expertise and local knowledge and ensure that its contribution helps deliver better results. Iceland has built close partnerships in partner countries with government entities, international organisations, the academic community, and non-governmental organisations. For example, Iceland has a strong partnership with the World Bank on geothermal energy in East Africa, where it aims to leverage expertise and scale-up investments (Box 5.2).

Box 5.2 The regional geothermal energy programme in East Africa draws on Iceland's expertise and builds partnerships for leverage and scale up

Iceland has over 100 years of experience in harnessing geothermal energy domestically and has shared this knowledge through its development co-operation for more than 40 years. In 2011 it partnered with the World Bank on a Geothermal Compact for East Africa. This compact has led to a Geothermal Exploration Project in East Africa's Rift Valley (2012-18) that draws on Iceland's expertise and matches it with the bank's convening power and financial resources. The project is open to 13 sub-Saharan African countries and aims to contribute to the compact's overarching objective of adding at least 200 MW of electricity from geothermal sources in the region in the next seven to fifteen years. To do so, the project's approach is to leverage and scale up activities by mitigating and distributing the risks associated with geothermal exploration. This approach helps clear bottlenecks which, in turn, promote investment in drilling projects and pipelines, notably from the private sector.

The project involves a range of stakeholders, such as the Nordic Development Fund, which co-finances exploration activities; the United Nations University Geothermal Programme, which provides training in geothermal use and policy; the United Nations Environmental Programme, the African Development Bank and the African Union, with which co-ordination can ensure alignment with regional objectives and enhance ownership.

Source: Government of Iceland and Nordic Development Fund (2012), *East African Rift Valley Geothermal Exploration Project (2013-2017)*.

Iceland's efforts to partner with the private sector in its geothermal activities are limited, but there is scope to reflect further on how Iceland might increase this co-operation. For example, in its multilateral activities, Iceland and other donors have agreed to a private

Chapter 5: Iceland's development co-operation delivery and partnerships

sector window in the International Development Association, to be channelled through the International Finance Corporation and Multilateral Investment Guarantee Agency. However, deepening partnerships with the private sector in this area would require a new vision for engaging with business through bilateral activities, as well as introducing new funding instruments and partnerships in a way that would not increase aid fragmentation (Chapter 1).

Iceland has strong relations with civil society but needs to sharpen its approach

Approximately 6% of Icelandic aid was allocated to civil society in 2013-14. Given Iceland's capacity limitations and those of its civil society, increasing its partnerships with civil society makes sense. The Ministry for Foreign Affairs works with a number of well-established organisations, mainly in the humanitarian domain (e.g. Icelandic Red Cross, Icelandic Church Aid, and SOS Children's Villages Iceland). In partner countries, Iceland also works with local civil society groups throughout the project cycle in order to increase local ownership and sustainability, which can be considered good practice.

Iceland has been streamlining its complex procedures for working and funding civil society organisations since 2010. Until 2014, Iceland had a special budget line for civil society co-operation open for application biannually for both development projects and humanitarian assistance. In order to learn from best practices the lines for humanitarian assistance and those for development co-operation were separated in 2015. This allows for a rapid response to humanitarian emergencies as they come up, while enabling civil society to submit applications for development grants once a year. Even though the rules for awarding grants to humanitarian projects are separate from the rules for development co-operation grants, they are based on DAC recommendations, Nordic good practice, the Good Humanitarian Donorship principles and other international rules. Iceland has been implementing multi-year funding arrangements and framework agreements to increase predictability, flexibility and the efficiency of its partnerships with civil society, while reducing transaction costs. All grant agreements now also include provisions on monitoring, reporting and evaluations, as well as on gender mainstreaming.

Notwithstanding this progress, Iceland still needs to define the rationale for selecting partners and principles which guides the nature of its partnerships with civil society. This is especially important if Iceland is to increase aid flows to civil society in the future. Icelandic civil society organisations need to be better integrated into the work of Iceland's field missions, and need to have an input into Iceland's policy-making process. A clearer vision could help share knowledge and raise awareness of development co-operation. Monitoring and evaluating civil society groups' activities would help to highlight the added value of working with them (OECD, 2011b); this is planned for 2017. The new International Development Cooperation Committee usefully brings together the key development co-operation stakeholders in Iceland, including non-government organisations (Chapter 4). However, Iceland needs to better capitalise on the committee's mandate to advise, provide oversight, and increase awareness and transparency of its activities.

Chapter 5: Iceland's development co-operation delivery and partnerships

Fragile states
Indicator: Delivery modalities and partnerships help deliver quality

Iceland is active in fragile states, and crisis management is an important axis of its development co-operation. Even if fragility is not one of the criteria that would lead Iceland to increase its assistance, Iceland will adapt its strategy and delivery mechanism in the event of a crisis or conflict. Iceland is supporting a range of partners and activities in crisis contexts, but the focus on gender equality and women's rights seems insufficient to coalesce all projects into a clear strategy for engagement. Building on its two existing country strategies, Iceland's development co-operation could benefit from an overall policy for engagement in crisis so that its instruments are coherently deployed in such contexts.

Solid country strategies could help guide a policy for fragile contexts

Crisis management is one of the key motivations for Iceland's development co-operation strategy, with implementation efforts focused on Afghanistan, the Middle East, and Ukraine. In line with its strategy, Iceland engages in crisis management or post-conflict contexts in two ways: by supporting multilateral partners or by deploying technical experts to international missions. Iceland is consistent in its focus on gender equality, and has developed a national action plan for the implementation of UN Security Council Resolution 1325 on Women, Peace and Security. This action plan structures Iceland's engagement across humanitarian, development and crisis management operations. It has strong rationale of supporting governance through gender equality programmes, and supporting reconstruction through expert deployment and financial support to multilateral organisations.

Iceland lacks an overarching strategy for engagement in crisis contexts. However, it does have very solid country strategies for crisis management in Afghanistan and the Middle East, which could potentially provide a good basis for a policy on crisis management and would ensure alignment with any future core strategic objectives for Iceland's work in crisis-affected areas.

Use of multilateral channels eases the burden on crisis-affected governments

Iceland works to improve the international response's coherence in fragile states through multilateral co-operation and UN-led peacebuilding efforts. At the World Humanitarian Summit in May 2016, Iceland committed to supporting the UN's conflict prevention capacities, particularly in terms of conflict analysis and the good offices function. Iceland has already contributed to the UN conflict prevention effort by seconding a member of staff to the UN political office in West Africa (UNOWA) and intends to support the United Nations in convening a World Prevention Forum by 2020. The World Bank, UNICEF and UN Women are privileged channels for Iceland's development co-operation in fragile contexts. This is good practice because it eases the burden on the affected country's government of managing multiple small development co-operation partners. When Iceland's support to multilateral organisations is complemented by the deployment of technical experts, it can also strengthen the affected government's capacities in improving women's rights and position while also improving Iceland's visibility.

Chapter 5: Iceland's development co-operation delivery and partnerships

Conflict is a stronger criterion than fragility for Iceland's development co-operation

Iceland is not using fragility to calibrate its delivery modality. Instead Iceland draws a distinction between conflict and non-conflict contexts to adjust its engagement. Iceland is engaged in conflict resolution programmes in Afghanistan, Ukraine and the Middle East, but also supports the UN's conflict prevention activities, as it did for instance in Western Africa. In such contexts, Iceland supports its multilateral or NGO partners and emphasises gender equality across all of its programmes. To complement its engagement, Iceland also deploys civilian technical expertise to the missions of multilateral organisations such as NATO or the Organisation for Security and Co-operation in Europe (OSCE) and to its UN development and humanitarian partners. Such delivery mechanisms support the statebuilding process as Iceland calibrates its aid according to its partner's capacity while staying in line with the international response.

Notes

1. Iceland unveiled its first five-year Statement of Fiscal Policy and a Fiscal Strategy Plan for the public sector in April 2016, approved in mid-2016.

2. Iceland's regional project on geothermal energy in the East African Rift Valley operates on a demand-driven basis and takes into account national development plans and priorities in the energy sector. However, Iceland maintains a parallel implementation unit in Reykjavik to run the project. This approach is serving Iceland well, given the exploratory nature of the project and the objective to reach up to 13 sub-Saharan African countries.

Chapter 5: Iceland's development co-operation delivery and partnerships

Bibliography

Government sources

Althingi (2016), "Five-year statement of fiscal policy and fiscal strategy plan for the public sector", (Icelandic only), Althingi, Reykjavik.

Althingi (2008), *Act on Iceland's International Development Cooperation (Act No. 121/2008)*, Althingi, Reykjavik, www.mfa.is/media/MFA_pdf/Act-on-Icelands-International-Development-Cooperation.pdf.

Government of Iceland (2016), "OECD DAC peer review of Iceland: memorandum", Reykjavik.

Government of Iceland (2015), *Forms and procedures for grants to civil society organisations for development aid and humanitarian assistance*, Government of Iceland, Reykjavik.

Government of Iceland (2014), *Evaluation of Health Sector Programme in Malawi*, Reykjavik.

Government of Iceland (2013), *Support to the Fisheries Sector of Mozambique 2013-2017 Programme Document Common Fund*, Government of Iceland, Reykjavik, www.iceida.is/media/verkefnagagnabanki/Support-to-the-Fisheries-Sector-of-Mozambique-2013-2017---Programme-Document-Common-Fund.pdf.

Government of Iceland (2012), *Mangochi Basic Services Programme 2012-2016,* Reykjavik.

Government of Iceland (2012), *Development Partnership in Buikwe, Uganda: Education Development in Fishing Communities,* Government of Iceland, Reykjavik.

Government of Iceland and Nordic Development Fund (2012), *East African Rift Valley Geothermal Exploration Project (2013-2017)*, Government of Iceland, Reykjavik.

ICEIDA (2012), *Guiding Principles for Addressing Environmental Issues*, Icelandic International Development Agency, Reykjavik, www.iceida.is/media/pdf/Guiding-Principles-for-Environmental-Issues.pdf.

ICEIDA (2011), *Vision and Procedures 2012-2014*, Icelandic International Development Agency, Reykjavik, Reykjavik, www.iceida.is/media/pdf/Vision-and-Procedures-2012-2014.pdf.

MFA (2013a), *Strategy for Iceland's International Development Cooperation 2013-2016*, Ministry for Foreign Affairs, Reykjavik.

MFA (2013b), *Women, Peace and Security: Iceland's National Action Plan for the Implementation of UN Security Council Resolution 1325 on Women, Peace and Security 2013–2016*, Ministry for Foreign Affairs, Reykjavik, www.mfa.is/media/fridargaeslan/UT-WomenPeaceSecurity-2013.pdf.

Other sources

OECD (2015), *Development Co-operation Report 2015: Making Partnerships Effective Coalitions for Action*, OECD Publishing, http://dx.doi.org/10.1787/dcr-2015-en.

OECD (2013), "Special Review of Iceland", OECD, Paris, www.oecd.org/dac/dac-global-relations/Iceland%20Special%20Review.pdf.

OECD (2011a), "Busan Partnership for Effective Development Co-operation", *Fourth High Level Forum on Aid Effectiveness, Busan, Republic of Korea, 29 November – 1 December 2011*, OECD, Paris, www.oecd.org/dac/effectiveness/49650173.pdf.

OECD (2011b), *Partnering with Civil Society: 12 Lessons from DAC Peer Reviews*, OECD, Paris, www.oecd.org/dac/peer-reviews/12%20Lessons%20Partnering%20with%20Civil%20Society.

Chapter 6: Results management and accountability of Iceland's development co-operation

Results-based management system

Indicator: A results-based management system is in place to assess performance on the basis of development priorities, objectives and systems of partner countries

Iceland monitors results to improve planning and implementation of its development co-operation and supports its bilateral partners' overall monitoring capacity by using their district-level results frameworks. Extending this results-orientation beyond bilateral to multilateral, regional and humanitarian activities would help Iceland to better account for all the results of its development programme.

Iceland has improved its results-based management efforts

Over the past five years, Iceland has stepped up its efforts to improve results-based management throughout its development co-operation programme. In preparation for the merger of Iceland's bilateral aid agency (ICEIDA) with the Ministry for Foreign Affairs the development co-operation act (Althingi, 2015), established a new holistic approach to results management with provisions for more active oversight by the Althingi (Chapter 4). In addition, at corporate level, from 2017 the Ministry for Foreign Affairs must submit a results framework to the Finance Ministry as part of a new five-year Statement of Fiscal Policy and Fiscal Strategy Plan for the public sector (Chapter 4; Althingi, 2016).[1]

As a result, Iceland is strengthening its work on managing for results, moving from monitoring inputs to outcomes and introducing results-based and outcome-oriented planning at corporate level. Expected outcomes for individual activities are developed in line with national development plans and Iceland is also examining how it might develop a common set of indicators across activities as a framework for its results management work. However, Iceland does not set out specific country-level goals or those global goals that partner countries prioritise. Overall, this approach is understandable for a donor with a small ODA budget working at district level, especially given that efforts to measure progress on global goals at the local level are in the early stages.[2] However, the Ministry for Foreign Affairs might reflect further on how it could use country and activity-level results more strategically for learning, communication, accountability and decision making to demonstrate how Iceland is achieving its overall development co-operation objectives. This does not mean trying to attribute Iceland's direct effort to the achievement of the global goals through its aid to partner countries. Rather, it implies demonstrating contribution to, and alignment with, those goals prioritised by its partners, particularly in areas where Iceland has a specific comparative advantage.

In both bilateral and multilateral programmes, Iceland's results reporting relies to a large extent on implementing partner frameworks. While this approach serves Iceland well in general, Iceland needs to find better ways to aggregate or synthesise information so that results only inform decisions at project level and at a strategic level. Overall, the quality of

Chapter 6: Results management and accountability of Iceland's development co-operation

Iceland's results frameworks is variable and, in some cases, weak (for example, with regard to the United Nations' University's training programmes).[3] To date, efforts for results-based management are most advanced in Iceland's bilateral programmes, where outcomes are monitored and managed at district level before, during and after intervention.

Iceland's partners are responsible for results

Iceland's approach to strengthening its results management is based on improving partner systems in ways that promote local accountability structures. Implementing partners are responsible for monitoring and reporting on results, which is good practice. In most cases, Iceland uses partner government results frameworks at district level. Expected results are agreed jointly; partners receive support to build their own monitoring and evaluation mechanisms; and results information is used to steer dialogue and to adapt projects as required – usually at output level. Iceland is aware of the challenges of improving its access to quality data, but makes clear trade-offs between access and capacity building. If data are not accessible, Iceland will sometimes request that district-level partners include additional indicators, while at the same time trying to avoid any increasing burden on partners. Iceland also uses information from national aid effectiveness reports to initiate discussions on effectiveness with partners. Iceland is currently considering how this progress on results-based management might now be extended to its multilateral and humanitarian co-operation.

Good use of partner monitoring capacities in fragile states, with spot checks from Reykjavik

Results-based management processes in fragile states imply good understanding of context, the associated risks and their consequences for implementation. In such cases, access to project and primary data is critical in order to measure, learn and adjust. Iceland has two distinct approaches to its results-based management in fragile states: (1) where local systems are operational, it uses existing district level results frameworks that are subject to occasional spot checks by the Ministry for Foreign Affairs, which is good practice and improves understanding of context at headquarters; and (2) where local systems are not operational, notably in crisis contexts, it relies on joint mechanisms using pooled funding and multilateral partners' monitoring expertise. In both cases, Iceland relies on partners' results monitoring mechanisms to consolidate and verify results before using this information to inform its own policy and strategic decisions.

Evaluation system

Indicator: The evaluation system is in line with the DAC evaluation principles

Iceland is strengthening its evaluation culture, taking a pragmatic approach and effectively integrating evaluation into the design of its bilateral programmes. The new evaluation policy presents an opportunity to extend evaluation to multilateral, humanitarian and civil society partners and increase oversight and knowledge sharing across Iceland's development co-operation.

Iceland has a new integrated evaluation unit and a new evaluation policy

Since it joined the Development Assistance Committee (DAC) in 2013, Iceland has taken a pragmatic approach to integrating evaluation into the design of its programmes. In addition to following OECD DAC norms and standards, Iceland's evaluations are also governed by the rules and procedures of the Icelandic National Audit Office on the treatment and management of development co-operation finance.

Following the merger of Iceland's bilateral and multilateral operations in early 2016, Iceland has adopted a new evaluation system with a single evaluation unit for all of

Chapter 6: Results management and accountability of Iceland's development co-operation

Iceland's development co-operation. Core responsibilities and duties of the unit include managing a wide range of evaluations and reviews, supervising and revising evaluation methodology and participating in international co-operation on related issues. However, extending the former bilateral agency's evaluation culture to other areas of Iceland's development co-operation is a top priority for the new unit. To support this new emphasis, Iceland has employed an additional evaluation expert and has strengthened the role of the new unit within the ministry (see Chapter 4). The ministry has also finalised a new evaluation policy to improve the quality of evaluations and broaden knowledge sharing in a way that is appropriate for Iceland's small-scale context (MFA, 2017).

Iceland is reinforcing the role of evaluations

Evaluations are conducted by external, independent consultants, who are recruited through an open tendering process in compliance with Icelandic State Procurement Bureau procedures. Nevertheless, bias and conflict of interest remains a risk for both evaluation design and management responses given the small number of ministry staff involved in aid management.

Iceland's new evaluation policy outlines the role of the evaluation unit as an internal function within the Ministry for Foreign Affairs, stating that the head of the evaluation unit shall report to the Director General for International Development, who reports to the Permanent Secretary. At the same time, the policy states that the Director of Evaluations is responsible for ensuring that the evaluations themselves are independent and that the evaluation function upholds DAC guidelines and procedures (MFA, 2017). As noted in the DAC's evaluation principles, impartiality and independence are often best achieved by separating the evaluation function from the line management responsible for planning and managing development assistance (OECD, 1991).

However, there are also some advantages in anchoring evaluation functions inside the aid management system, particularly in terms of management of knowledge gained from evaluations. In this case, the evaluation function should report to a sufficiently high level of the management structure and every effort should be made to avoid compromising the evaluation process and its results.

Now that Iceland has decided on a unified reporting structure for both multilateral and bilateral co-operation, it will be important to ensure that activities financed by Iceland's ODA outside the responsibility of the Ministry for Foreign Affairs (e.g. in-donor refugee programmes) are also subject to evaluation.

Iceland's evaluations strengthen mutual accountability and partner capacity

From the outset, Iceland's bilateral reviews and external evaluations are planned for, funded and shared with partners to ensure mutual accountability and promote lessons. Evaluations can be carried out at different stages of the programme cycles, from design to mid-term to final and ex-post evaluations. Cross-cutting issues of gender and environment are addressed in all evaluations, irrespective of whether they are a specific programme objective. However, to date, Iceland has not undertaken thematic evaluations in their own right -- for example on gender – due to timing issues, preferring to wait for the 2013-16 strategy period to end.

All bilateral programme and project documents include an end-of-programme/project evaluation, a mid-term review, a schedule and a budget. These plans are developed at headquarters and discussed at the field level and with partners, with a current focus on development outcomes. Where possible, Iceland also undertakes joint evaluations (for example with Norway on joint work in fisheries in Mozambique). While Iceland does not regularly undertake ex-post impact evaluations, those that it has commissioned have shown positive and sustainable impacts.[4]

Agreements with civil society and international organisations all contain evaluation provisions. Multilateral partnerships are generally evaluated through use of multi-stakeholder mechanisms (i.e. the Multilateral Organization Performance Assessment Network, MOPAN[5]) or other bilateral donor assessments. Given the small size of Iceland's contributions to these organisations, this approach makes sense.

Iceland's new evaluation policy (MFA, 2016) sets out provisions for an indicative multi-year plan to manage evaluations across Iceland's development co-operation portfolio. However, given the capacity constraints inherent in Iceland's development co-operation, this planning instrument would also benefit from the development of detailed selection criteria to assist in prioritising evaluations. These criteria could be usefully included in or annexed to Iceland's forthcoming action plan for development co-operation. This process should also help Iceland to plan for evaluation costs in advance.

Institutional learning

Indicator: Evaluations and appropriate knowledge management systems are used as management tools

Iceland is committed to improving its institutional learning, but has some way to go to effectively marshal its resources and knowledge for useful knowledge management and planning.

Iceland uses evaluations in decision making

Iceland relies heavily on evaluations to support decision-making on its development co-operation. This process takes place informally, through in-house discussions and follow-up action. Evaluations are first shared within the ministry, then with partners, before being submitted to the Development Co-operation Committee and published on the ministry's website and other media. Cross-country lessons are also shared, for example from Malawi to Uganda on financial management programmes and monitoring frameworks. In all, there is ample anecdotal evidence of the impact of bilateral evaluations on decision-making, including in supporting programme extension or, alternatively, in withdrawing from activities with poor development impact.[6] However, a more formal approach to learning from, and using, evaluations might further strengthen Iceland's use of evaluation findings. For example, mid-term reviews often occur too late to influence changes in the second half of a programme and there is no simple system in place to track management follow-up after evaluations are released. Iceland's thematic evaluations and reviews (e.g. on gender) also present a good opportunity to extend established evaluation practice in the bilateral programme to multilateral, humanitarian and civil society partnerships and to increase oversight and knowledge across Iceland's development co-operation.

Iceland is formalising its knowledge management systems.

A previous review of Iceland's development co-operation (OECD, 2013) has highlighted the need for Iceland to improve its knowledge management, either through a formal system or a strategy to ensure successful informal knowledge transfer and institutional learning. While a more informal approach has worked well for the bilateral programme in the past, the new integrated evaluation policy and indicative multi-year plan should improve oversight and knowledge-sharing across Iceland's development co-operation portfolio.[7] In addition, these new mechanisms could help share knowledge with partner countries and civil society organisations. This is particularly important when preparing the extension of

Chapter 6: Results management and accountability of Iceland's development co-operation

programmes, new programmes or programme exits, where the results of evaluations can form a critical input into preparatory work. In developing this new system, building in feedback loops from partners, including civil society organisations, would help both headquarters and local staff to use the system for forward planning.

Communication, accountability and development awareness
Indicator: The member communicates development results transparently and honestly

Iceland is committed to transparency and is making efforts to extend the quality of its communications to parliamentarians, civil society organisations, schools, academia and the private sector. Following the merger of its development co-operation administrations, Iceland's new communication strategy takes this work to a new level, using social media and challenge funding to strengthen the engagement of a broad audience. The 2030 Agenda for Sustainable Development presents a further opportunity to enhance communication on global citizenship and the interdependence among Icelandic interests, development goals and global public goods.

Iceland is a transparent donor	Iceland is a transparent and credible donor, publishing much information about its development co-operation on its website and making documents available at the Ministry for Foreign Affairs. While these efforts stalled in the first half of 2016 following the merger of the bilateral and multilateral development co-operation arms (Chapter 4), Iceland is now bringing its development co-operation website up-to-date, with the aim of publishing all programmes and partnerships.
	In addition, Iceland's development co-operation act requires the Minister for Foreign Affairs to report development results to the Althingi every two years, as well as provide regular updates to the Foreign Affairs and Finance committees. Given the delay in forming a new government following the national elections, it is currently unclear when the next report on development co-operation results will be published or when the minister will next report to the Althingi on development co-operation. However, the Ministry for Foreign Affairs expects this to occur in 2017 at the same time as the new development co-operation policy and action plan go to parliament for decision.
	Despite these delays, this level of transparency enhances Iceland's accountability towards its partners, the general public and parliament, as evidenced by an increasing number of visitors to the Ministry for Foreign Affairs development co-operation website (www.iceida.is) and growing audience on social media. Iceland is now well placed to push this agenda further by supporting its partners to reach the same degree of transparency.
Iceland could provide a better overview of its development co-operation efforts	Iceland communicates the results of its development co-operation to major stakeholders (including taxpayers, lawmakers, partners and beneficiaries) through its website and other media, using development results gathered through its own and partner systems. The ministry's website hosts a comprehensive database of programme and project documents, evaluation and reviews and makes efforts to communicate on risks and negative outcomes (for example, it has published negative evaluations on outcomes of its fisheries programmes in the past). However, Iceland could further improve its reporting to stakeholders on the overall results and outcomes of its development co-operation, providing concise information that demonstrates results achieved and challenges faced.

Chapter 6: Results management and accountability of Iceland's development co-operation

In further developing its approach to communicating results, Iceland can learn from others on how to make more strategic use of country-based evidence on the results of its programme and its impact on people in developing countries. One recent positive development on this front is the re-launch of ICEIDA's popular weekly magazine, *Heimsljós*, which uses storytelling and social media to communicate the results of Iceland's development co-operation activities. It also explains why some programmes have not succeeded or have needed to change course. Furthermore, Iceland's new International Committee for Development Co-operation can play a useful role in deepening communication on the results of Iceland's development co-operation efforts in line with its mandate to regularly update the Althingi's Foreign Affairs Committee (Althingi, 2015).

A draft communications strategy targets young people

Iceland recognises it must do more to improve public and political understanding of its development co-operation. A survey of public opinion on development, conducted in 2013, showed overwhelming support for development co-operation, but little knowledge about it. To improve communication efforts, Iceland's Ministry for Foreign Affairs is drafting a new development communications strategy that aims to take accountability and public awareness to a new level. This draft strategy identifies a range of approaches, such as using social media, school education programmes and challenge funding, to increase development awareness among Icelanders, particularly young people (Box 6.1). Meanwhile, Iceland's new Development Co-operation Committee has a mandate to raise development awareness, though it has yet to define how these efforts should proceed and how this can complement the MFA's communication activities.

Iceland could also strengthen its efforts to communicate results by working more with its non-government organisation partners to provide the Icelandic public and parliament with targeted information on development results to support informed discussion. The ministry already has a contract with the United Nations Association in Iceland and the national committees of UN Women and UNICEF to raise public awareness of development issues. Until 2014, the former ICEIDA also organised a week-long programme of events with a different development co-operation theme each year, entitled "Development Cooperation Bears Fruit". Iceland could consider the merits of extending these efforts to all its home-based non-government organisations, potentially using the global goals to drive new momentum. Future surveys of public attitudes on development co-operation, scheduled to take place every two years starting in 2017, should confirm whether Iceland's efforts to improve public awareness of development issues are working.

Chapter 6: Results management and accountability of Iceland's development co-operation

> **Box 6.1 Iceland's new communications strategy**
>
> Iceland's draft five-year communications strategy (2017-21) and associated action plan (2017-19) aim to promote development awareness, especially among young people. In addition to strengthening existing communication tools – such as the project database on the website, public attitudes survey and weekly newsletter – new budgeting measures and communications initiatives include:
>
> - ring-fencing 1% of the ODA budget for communicating Iceland's development results and increasing public awareness of development issues
>
> - publishing a new text book on global development issues in association with the UN Association of Iceland and rolling out an education programme on development co-operation for schools
>
> - co-operating with the Icelandic Film Centre to make an annual documentary on development issues
>
> - setting up a challenge fund for innovative and/or influential media and education efforts on Iceland's development co-operation, aimed at film-makers, journalists, teachers and writers
>
> - increasing the use of social media (with 90% of partners and Iceland's development co-operation audience accessing information through social media platforms).
>
> - designing a new-look development co-operation website, which is more user-friendly and provides targeted information on development results.
>
> One of the biggest communication challenges for Iceland's development co-operation is reaching the Althingi (Iceland's Parliament), as recognised by a number of Icelandic parliamentarians themselves. While Iceland's development co-operation act stipulates that results must be reported to the Althingi, and while there was considerable discussion on the merits of integrating ICEDA's functions within the Ministry for Foreign Affairs[8], to date there has been little focus from the Althingi on Iceland's development results or the role Iceland can play to support the Sustainable Development Goals. Working through Iceland's recently appointed Committee on International Development Cooperation, which has oversight of all Iceland's development co-operation and includes parliamentarians from all parties, could be further explored as a potential entry point for this communication with the Althingi.
>
> *Source:* MFA (2016), Interviews in Reykjavik, "OECD-DAC peer review of Iceland 2017: memorandum"; MFA (2016)

Notes

1. This directive applies to all Iceland's line ministries. For the Ministry for Foreign Affairs, the Directorate for International Development Co-operation is a separate expenditure area within the ministry's plan and is held accountable by the Finance Ministry for development co-operation results.

2. Current efforts to "localise" the sustainable development goals (i.e. measure progress against each goal at district/local level) are still at an early stage. However, Iceland may be able to draw on such work in the future. Further information is available at http://unhabitat.org/roadmap-for-localizing-the-sdgs-implementation-and-monitoring-at-subnational-level/.

3. The forthcoming review of the impact of UNU programmes in developing countries is particularly timely and measurement of country-level results will help Iceland to identify how these allocations can better align with, and contribute to, the strategic objectives of Iceland's development co-operation (see Box 2.1 in Chapter 2).

4. To date, Iceland has completed two impact evaluations. The first was an ex-post evaluation of the impact of 20 years' work in the fisheries sector in Namibia, conducted five years after exiting the country. The second was the recent impact evaluation of the Monkey Bay Community Hospital in Malawi. Both evaluations found positive impacts on the poorest communities, with benefits that were sustained after Icelandic aid was withdrawn, or – in the Malawi case – when Icelandic aid switched from direct project implementation to devolution of responsibilities to the district level.

5. Iceland is not a member of MOPAN, but relies on the assessments undertaken and publicised by MOPAN to inform its decision making.

6. Iceland's evaluations in Uganda and Malawi have supported programme extensions, while another on education in Mozambique promoted a decision to exit the sector. For example, a number of problems with data collection identified in the 2014 midterm review of the Malawi district-level services programme have been being incorporated into the extension programme for 2016-2020.

7. The planned gender strategy also presents an opportunity to extend evaluation to multilateral, humanitarian and civil society partners and increase oversight and knowledge sharing across Iceland's development co-operation.

8. The Minister of Foreign Affairs reports to the parliament on an annual basis in March each year on the ministry's work, including on international development. The Ministry for Foreign Affairs also meets regularly with the Foreign Affairs committee. In addition, changes to the Act were discussed for an estimated 60 hours in the period leading up to the integration of ICEDA and the Ministry for Foreign Affairs.

Chapter 6: Results management and accountability of Iceland's development co-operation

Bibliography

Althingi (2016), "Five-year statement of fiscal policy and fiscal strategy plan for the public sector", (in Icelandic), Althingi, Reykjavik.

Althingi (2015), *Act 122/2015: amendment to Act No 121/2008*, Althingi, Reykjavik.

Althingi (2012), *Act 161/2012: amendment to Act No 121/2008*, Althingi, Reykjavik.

Althingi (2008), *Act on Iceland's International Development Cooperation (Act No. 121/2008)*, Althingi, Reykjavik, www.mfa.is/media/MFA_pdf/Act-on-Icelands-International-Development-Cooperation.pdf.

Government of Iceland (2011), "A parliamentary resolution on a Strategy for Iceland's international development co-operation 2011-2014", Government of Iceland, Reykjavik.

ICEIDA (2015), "Monitoring and evaluation for ICEIDA: introduction for staff", Icelandic International Development Agency, Reykjavik.

ICEIDA (2013), Survey of Public Attitudes on Development (in Icelandic), Icelandic International Development Agency, Reykjavik, www.iceida.is/media/pdf/1307_Throunarsamvinna_final.pdf.

MFA (forthcoming), *Policy for Iceland's International Development Cooperation (2017-2021)*, draft, Ministry for Foreign Affairs, Reykjavik.

MFA (2016), *Evaluation Policy for Iceland's Development Cooperation*, Ministry for Foreign Affairs, Reykjavik.

MFA (2016), "OECD-DAC peer review of Iceland 2017: memorandum", Ministry for Foreign Affairs, Reykjavik.

MFA (2013), *Strategy for Iceland's International Development Cooperation (2013-2016)*, (Icelandic only, highlights available in English), Ministry for Foreign Affairs, Reykjavik, www.mfa.is/media/throunarsamvinna/MFA-StrategyforIcelandsDevelopmentCooperation-2013-2016.pdf.

Mkamanga, G. (2014), "Mangochi Basic Services Programme 2012-2016: mid-term evaluation", Final Report, www.iceida.is/media/pdf/MBSP-MID-TERM-EVALUATION_FINAL.pdf.

Other sources

OECD (2016a), "Providers' use of results information for accountability, communication, direction and learning. Survey results, Iceland survey response", August 2016, OECD, Paris. www.oecd.org/dac/peer-reviews/Providers'_use_of_results_information_for_accountability_communication_direction_and_learning.pdf.

OECD (2016b), *Evaluation Systems in Development Co-operation: 2016 Review*, OECD Publishing, http://dx.doi.org/10.1787/9789264262065-en.

OECD (2014), *Engaging with the Public: Twelve Lessons from DAC Peer Reviews*, OECD Development Co-operation Peer Reviews, OECD Publishing, http://dx.doi.org/10.1787/9789264226739-en.

OECD (2013), "Special review of Iceland", OECD, Paris, www.oecd.org/dac/dac-global-relations/Iceland%20Special%20Review.pdf.

Chapter 7: Iceland's humanitarian assistance

Strategic framework
Indicator: Clear political directives and strategies for resilience, response and recovery

Iceland's overall policy framework for humanitarian aid is solid and driven by international standards. The country makes the best use of its limited resources and maximises its impact and visibility by deploying technical experts to UN agencies' field missions. Iceland pays great attention to gender equality throughout its humanitarian and development assistance strategies. This focus is clear and gives Iceland's policy greater clout and coherence.

Iceland aligns itself with global policy trends

The humanitarian policy framework derives from the 2008 act on Iceland's international development co-operation (Althingi, 2008) and the Development Cooperation Strategy 2013-2016 (MFA, 2013). The humanitarian strategy is driven by international humanitarian law and the Good Humanitarian Donorship principles (GHD, 2003). Even though it did not endorse the Grand Bargain at the World Humanitarian Summit in May 2016, Iceland is already implementing some of its provisions. For instance, it is increasing the predictability of its funds and providing core funding to its multilateral partners. Doing so brings Iceland in line with global humanitarian policy trends.

Iceland is consistent in its orientation from the emergency to the recovery phase

Iceland channels most of its humanitarian aid through both core and earmarked contributions to UN agencies, which themselves link emergency response and development programmes. In the Middle East, for instance, Iceland has a long-standing partnership with the UN Relief and Works Agency for Palestine Refugees in the Near East (UNRWA).[1] Such long-term support helps agencies to formulate transition programmes for the people they help. Focusing on gender equality as a cross-cutting issue also allows Iceland to be consistent in its programme orientation, from the emergency response through to the recovery phase.

Iceland should ensure its investment in resilience is sustained by partner government finance

Iceland strengthens the resilience of vulnerable communities and builds national capacity through its development co-operation, which is seen as a better tool than humanitarian aid for building resilience. This is good practice, and helps to ensure sustainable impact while also preserving the relatively small humanitarian budget for other priorities. Iceland has a coherent approach which brings natural resource preservation, education and health together as key development sectors, since they influence the capacity of populations to cope with natural hazards or economic shocks. In the Middle East, for instance, Iceland has supported local efforts to develop a natural disaster emergency response plan. In addition, support at sub-national level to social sectors, like health in Malawi and Uganda, make a direct contribution to the country's resilience if it is carefully integrated within government priorities and systems. However, programme ownership by national authorities in those countries must go beyond the formal integration into national priorities – adequate finance must also be mobilised in order to sustain the gains made from development co-operation investments. Iceland, along with other donors, should ensure this happens.

Chapter 7: Iceland's humanitarian assistance

The limited humanitarian budget is complemented by seconding expert to partners

Iceland's humanitarian budget has grown over the years – from USD 1.03 million in 2012[2] to USD 5.8 million in 2015.[3] The latter included a special USD 3.4 million allocation for the Syria crisis. Iceland also has the flexibility to increase funds to match its strategic objectives when responding to a large-scale crisis. For example, late in 2015 the government committed ISK 2 billion (USD 15 million) to help respond to the refugee crisis in the Middle East (Government of Iceland, 2015).[4] The Ministry for Foreign Affairs has earmarked ISK 750 million (USD 6.55 million) from this envelope to support international bodies and NGOs over a 15-month period.[5] Iceland is also a recurring contributor to the Central Emergency Response Fund (CERF), and has increased its annual contribution threefold, to reach USD 300 000 in 2016. In this way, Iceland makes good use of its resources and is consistent with its own strategy to support an UN-led humanitarian response. It is also in line with its commitment at the World Humanitarian Summit to strengthen its support to CERF and country-based pooled funds (Agenda for Humanity, 2016). Iceland's contribution to humanitarian response, however, is not only financial. The Iceland Crisis Response Unit (ICRU) has standby partnership agreements with several UN agencies.[6] Through this mechanism, Iceland is able to provide human resources to its partners. Providing such expertise to its partners is an efficient and visible way for Iceland to complement limited financial resources.

Effective programme design

Indicator: Programmes target the highest risk to life and livelihood

With limited field presence and no early warning capacity, Iceland makes good use of its partners' information flows in order to programme its humanitarian aid. Iceland's humanitarian assistance is organised so that it fits with its preferred multilateral channel, responds to appeals, and contributes to UN-led pooled funds. While focused on a limited number of crises, Iceland's assistance retains the flexibility to respond to small-scale disasters and also maintains a competent search and rescue team for sudden onset disasters.

Iceland is a good system player, making use of its partners' information and tools

Iceland relies primarily on its partnership with the UN agencies and other multilateral organisations to inform its humanitarian funding, notably by responding to appeals from multilateral organisations. Iceland's humanitarian aid is provided to a limited number of crises. For instance in 2014, 12 out of 19 projects supported two humanitarian crises in the Middle East. Additionally, Iceland makes good use of its partnerships with the International Committee of the Red Cross (ICRC), the International Federation of the Red Cross (IFRC) and to a lesser extent its NGO partners, to respond to crises that do not usually receive much humanitarian funding. For instance, in 2015 Iceland supported responses to small-scale disasters, such as the floods in Serbia and drought in Namibia. As the share of humanitarian funds allocated to pooled funds is due to increase in the coming years, Iceland increasingly delegates funding decisions to the managers of these pooled funds. By taking such decisions, Iceland is acting as a good system player, but should then pay specific attention to programme results.

Chapter 7: Iceland's humanitarian assistance

The search and rescue team is a valuable asset for Iceland

While Iceland mostly uses its partners as sources of information in order to programme its general humanitarian assistance, Icelandic staff are more directly involved in responses to sudden onset natural disasters. Iceland maintains an international search and rescue team, ready to be deployed at short notice. These teams are mobilised by the Iceland Crisis Response Unit (ICRU) through the United Nations Disaster Assessment and Coordination (UNDAC).[7] The Iceland search and rescue team is specialised in urban search and rescue, which has proven to be a valuable asset in major earthquake responses, such as in Haiti and Nepal.

Iceland's support of well-designed pooled funds can contribute to participation by affected communities

Iceland believes its focus on gender equality across all of its humanitarian funding helps promote women's participation throughout the programme cycle. Aside from this, Icelandic humanitarian assistance is mostly channelled through multilateral organisations and pooled funds, which prevents Iceland from directly supporting or interacting with national or local responders. However, Iceland is enabling the shift of resources to affected communities when it supports country-based pooled funds that are accessible to national NGOs, and when it uses unconditional cash-based interventions as a delivery channel. Better support to well-designed country-based pooled funds will increase participation by affected communities and ensure assistance better tailored to people's needs.

Effective delivery, partnerships and instruments

Indicator: Delivery modalities and partnerships help deliver quality

Iceland primarily relies on its partnership with multilateral organisations to deliver assistance from the emergency phase through to recovery. It has built solid partnerships with the main UN humanitarian agencies and complements its limited funding by deploying technical experts to its partners. Partnership with humanitarian NGOs is more limited, but is to be strengthened with a new partnership agreement. When engaging in protracted crises, even if the scope remains limited, humanitarian assistance could be more strategically aligned with development or peacebuilding instruments.

Iceland has tools for protracted crises and recovery but needs to deploy them strategically

Iceland contributes to UN-led country-based pooled funds.[8] Such mechanisms are of increasing interest to Iceland, which committed to provide more support for them at the World Humanitarian Summit (Agenda for Humanity, 2016). Such support promotes coherence and good practice for a donor with limited funds and capacity. However, Iceland does not use its funding tools evenly from one crisis to another. In the Middle East, Iceland makes use of a broad range of instruments, including expert deployment, to support humanitarian assistance, disaster risk management, social services and reconstruction. Conversely, in other protracted crises the response is much narrower: in Syria, Iceland uses only humanitarian aid whereas in Afghanistan it uses only small-scale development and security instruments. If Iceland wishes to increase its engagement in the Middle East and the refugee crisis, as shown by the extra budgetary allocation in late 2015, it could consider complementing its humanitarian assistance with development co-operation programming, for instance in the social sector. This would help align its humanitarian responses with its governance and reconstruction strategic axes.

Chapter 7: Iceland's humanitarian assistance

Multilateral delivery mechanisms facilitate rapid response

Favouring a UN-led humanitarian response, Iceland uses multilateral channels as primary mechanisms for both crisis response and recovery. Iceland is a small but regular contributor to the Central Emergency Response Fund (CERF).[9] Contributing to the CERF supports an early response to any new humanitarian crisis, and is therefore an adequate early response mechanism for a donor with limited capacity. Iceland also has standby partnership agreements with the main humanitarian agencies, allowing it to second technical expertise or to send search and rescue teams at short notice when requested by its partners.

Partnership with multilaterals is solid, while Iceland is still refining its work with NGOs

Iceland knows its budget can have greatest impact when it is added to larger financial flows. This is why its preference of working with multilateral agencies and pooled funds is sound practice. Iceland has partnership agreements with the main humanitarian agencies, who generally value Iceland's flexible funding – often core or only lightly earmarked – and its active policy role.[12] Partnerships with NGOs are more complex. Iceland is working on its partnerships with NGOs, including clarifying the selection process. However, some NGO partners told the peer review team they still believe this process should be clearer and more formal. Iceland is currently preparing a framework partnership agreement to further regulate its relationship with NGOs; this process should be used to clarify and improve delivery of aid through NGOs.

Iceland reinforces its policy messages through the Nordic donors group

Iceland is aware that co-ordination with other donors can maximise the impact of its limited resources. It co-operates with other Nordic nations to channel messages to its multilateral partners, including during an annual meeting with UN agencies such as the United Nations Office for the Coordination of Humanitarian Affairs (OCHA) and the World Food Programme. Iceland is also part of the Nordic plus group,[13] which gives more weight to Iceland's position and priorities than its financial contribution would normally allow. Additionally, when interacting with other donors and partners, a constant focus on gender equality and women's rights in crises gives credibility to Iceland at the policy level, whereas this is less the case at the operational level without field presence or significant funding flows.

Chapter 7: Iceland's humanitarian assistance

Organisation fit for purpose

Indicator: Systems, structures, processes and people work together effectively and efficiently

Ministries co-ordinate closely to manage refugees arriving in Iceland. The merger of the development agency and the Ministry for Foreign Affairs is an opportunity for greater coherence in Iceland's engagement in crisis contexts. Civilian deployment to peacebuilding missions and to humanitarian partners is a trademark of Iceland's assistance. The role of the Icelandic Crisis Response Unit could be strengthened to make it the co-ordinating entity for crisis response, including humanitarian aid.

ICRU could take on a co-ordination role for operation and deployment in crisis areas	A strong co-ordination mechanism exists between the ministries for foreign affairs, welfare and interior; municipal bodies (which receive subsidies to cover housing costs); and the Icelandic Red Cross in order to manage refugee arrivals and organise asylum requests and integration in Iceland. Internationally, all deployments to crisis contexts are managed by the Iceland Crisis Response Unit (ICRU) within the Ministry for Foreign Affairs. ICRU's role still needs to be clarified. Created in 2001 to manage deployment within international peacekeeping and peacebuilding missions, the scope of ICRU's activities has subsequently increased. Under the responsibility of the Directorate for International Development Co-operation within the ministry, ICRU has now a dual mandate: it deploys staff to security-related missions, but also sends staff to humanitarian or UN development missions. While not all of these deployments and activities are reported as ODA, they are all related to crisis response. Provided that funding streams between development ODA and other security funding sources are clearly demarcated, ICRU could take on an overall co-ordinating role within the ministry for all interventions in crisis areas, including humanitarian aid. This would allow for a more coherent Icelandic engagement strategy in all crisis contexts.
Only civilian personnel are deployed to international missions	Although it does not have armed forces to deploy, Iceland is part of NATO peacekeeping missions, for example in Afghanistan where it deploys civilian personnel. Deployments to international missions and humanitarian aid missions, including civil protection during natural disasters, are managed by ICRU within the Ministry of Foreign Affairs. Before deployment, all seconded personnel receive training on the Geneva conventions and security related issues, and other specific training as required for the deployment. This is good practice.
Skilled staff manage an increasing portfolio	Three members of staff manage Iceland's humanitarian aid and ICRU's deployments within the Ministry for Foreign Affairs. As most of Iceland's humanitarian aid is delivered through multilateral channels, the workload is heavy but manageable for these staff. However, the increased budget in 2015 (Section 7.1.4) has increased the grant administration workload. Bearing this in mind, Iceland should ensure humanitarian staff continue to have sufficient time to maintain and nurture partnerships with donor groups, multilateral organisations and NGOs.

Chapter 7: Iceland's humanitarian assistance

Results, learning and accountability
Indicator: Results are measured and communicated, and lessons learnt

Iceland primarily supports its multilateral partners with light or no earmarking. While this is good humanitarian donorship practice, it makes it difficult to measure impact or results at the project level and to communicate about Iceland's role in crisis contexts. Evaluating the effectiveness of its long-lasting engagement in Afghanistan and the Middle East could help assessing the need for organisational changes.

Evaluating Iceland's long-term humanitarian engagement is strategically important	To date, humanitarian aid has not been specifically targeted in Iceland's evaluation plans. However, Iceland does now intend to evaluate its humanitarian programmes. This is good: Iceland has been intervening in Afghanistan and the Middle East for more than a decade, using several of its development co-operation and humanitarian tools, but has never reviewed this engagement. Such a process could help Iceland to clarify its objectives in crisis settings, including humanitarian assistance, and determine the best role for the ICRU in the new ministry architecture.
Monitoring the impact of programmes remains a challenge	Iceland assesses its partners' performance through MOPAN and partners' own evaluations and self-reporting. However, this system makes it difficult for Iceland to grasp the real results of its humanitarian funding. According to the Ministry for Foreign Affairs project final reports are on average 83 days late,[14] which prevents them from feeding into follow-up funding decisions. Donor field visits are organised by UN agencies within the frame of the Nordic donors group, but these are not examples of independent monitoring. Iceland could consider joining forces with other Nordic plus donor group members to participate in or organise joint independent field visits.
Communication of humanitarian activities is not sufficient	Communication with the public on humanitarian issues has improved, notably in relation to the Syrian crisis and other recent large-scale humanitarian crises when news stories on these issues dominated the website of Iceland's Ministry for Foreign Affairs and occupied a significant space in general media reporting. However, information on humanitarian activities and related budgets has not always been easy to find on the ministry's website. With public opinion largely positive, notably on the response to the refugee crisis,[15] Iceland could do more to improve how it communicates its activities in crisis contexts more generally, drawing on ICEIDA's experience in this area.

Chapter 7: Iceland's humanitarian assistance

Notes

1. In 2015, Iceland was ranked 32 out of 52 donors to UNRWA.
2. OECD Creditor Reporting System, 21 Sept 2016. http://stats.oecd.org/Index.aspx?datasetcode=CRS1.
3. Provided by Ministry of Foreign Affairs, 5 January 2017.
4. In September 2015, the government proposed USD 15 million in special funds for support to refugees and asylum seekers in the Middle East over a 15-month period (MFA, 2015).
5. As a result, Iceland's humanitarian budget reached USD 3.9 million in 2015 (Government of Iceland, 2016).
6. Namely the World Food Programme (WFP), UNICEF, UNHCR, OCHA, UNRWA and UN Women.
7. See more about UNDAC at: www.unocha.org/what-we-do/coordination-tools/undac/overview.
8. Iceland was the 16th contributor to UN country-based pooled funds in 2015 with a USD 800 000 allocation.
9. Iceland was the 35th contributor to the CERF in 2016, and has made a stable USD 100 000 annual contribution since 2014 (www.unocha.org/cerf/donors/donorspage).
10. Irrespective of when a crisis occurs in the year, the partner must stop its accounting on 31st December and report on its activity and expenditure before submitting a follow-up call for proposal. There is no certainty that the follow-up proposal will be retained by the selection committee. If selected, the NGO has to meet its expenditure between the 1st January and the signature date of the new contract, as expenses are not eligible retroactively. This puts partners at financial, operational and security risks as not all field costs can be stopped by 31 December.
11. This is a first attempt at supporting multiannual humanitarian projects. It requires the NGO to deliver a first financial and technical report by 31 January 2016 and second one by 31st January 2017. This protocol has been primarily used in development projects (Polish Aid, 2016a).
12. MFA (ICRU) has a stand-by partnership agreement with OCHA, WFP and UNICEF. MFA has a framework agreement with WFP.
13. The Nordic plus group consists of the Nordic countries: Denmark, Sweden, Finland, Iceland and Norway; plus the United Kingdom, the Netherlands and Ireland.
14. Interview with the Ministry of Foreign Affairs, 8 September 2016, Reykjavik.
15. A survey conducted for Amnesty in Iceland in July and August 2016 showed that 85% of its respondents were in favour of hosting more Syrian refugees in Iceland over the next few months (www.maskina.is/en). A similar survey in October 2016 indicated that 73% of Icelanders were in favour of receiving refugees (http://ruv.is/frett/73-prosent-hlynnt-mottoku-fleiri-flottamanna).

Chapter 7: Iceland's humanitarian assistance

Bibliography

Government sources

Althingi (2008), Act on Iceland's International Development Cooperation (Act No. 121/2008), Althingi, Reykjavik, www.mfa.is/media/MFA_pdf/Act-on-Icelands-International-Development-Cooperation.pdf.

Government of Iceland (2016a), Foreign Minister's report to Althingi, the Parliament of Iceland: www.mfa.is/media/gunnar-bragi/FM-Report-to-Parliament-2016_EN-summary.pdf.

Government of Iceland (2016b), "OECD DAC peer review of Iceland: memorandum", Government of Iceland, Reykjavik.

Government of Iceland (2015), "Two billion ISK reserved for support to refugees and asylum seekers", Prime Minister's Office press release, 20 September, https://eng.forsaetisraduneyti.is/news-and-articles/nr/8594.

MFA (forthcoming), Policy for Iceland's Development Co-operation 2017-21, Ministry for Foreign Affairs, Reykjavik.

MFA (2013), Strategy for Iceland's International Development Cooperation (2013-2016), Ministry for Foreign Affairs, Reykjavik, www.mfa.is/media/throunarsamvinna/MFA-StrategyforIcelandsDevelopmentCooperation-2013-2016.pdf.

Other sources

Agenda for Humanity (2016), "World Humanitarian Summit donors' commitments", PACT database, www.agendaforhumanity.org/explore-commitments/indv-commitments/?combine=Iceland,

GHD (2003), 23 Principles and Good Practice of Humanitarian Donorship, Declaration made in Stockholm, 16-17 June, Good Humanitarian Donorship initiative, www.ghdinitiative.org/ghd/gns/principles-good-practice-of-ghd/principles-good-practice-ghd.html

Annex A: OECD/DAC standard suite of tables

Table A.1 Total financial flows

USD million at current prices and exchange rates

Iceland	2001-05	2006-10	2011	2012	2013	2014	2015
							Net disbursements
Total official flows	**18**	**40**	**26**	**26**	**35**	**37**	**40**
Official development assistance	**18**	**40**	**26**	**26**	**35**	**37**	**40**
Bilateral	12	29	20	21	29	31	31
Multilateral	6	11	6	5	6	6	9
Other official flows	-	-	-	-	-	-	-
Bilateral	-	-	-	-	-	-	-
Multilateral	-	-	-	-	-	-	-
Net Private Grants	-	-	-	-	-	-	-
Private flows at market terms	-	-	-	-	-	-	0
Bilateral: *of which*	-	-	-	-	-	-	0
Direct investment	-	-	-	-	-	-	0
Export credits	-	-	-	-	-	-	-
Multilateral	-	-	-	-	-	-	-
Total flows	**18**	**40**	**26**	**26**	**35**	**37**	**40**
for reference:							
ODA (at constant 2014 USD million)	19	40	28	30	38	37	42
ODA (as a % of GNI)	0.16	0.29	0.20	0.20	0.23	0.22	0.24
Total flows (as a % of GNI) (a)	0.16	0.29	0.20	0.20	0.23	0.22	0.24
ODA to and channelled through NGOs							
- In USD million	-	-	1	2	3	3	5
- In percentage of total net ODA	-	-	5	8	8	7	12
- DAC countries' average % of total net ODA	9	7	9	13	13	13	13

a. To countries eligible for ODA.

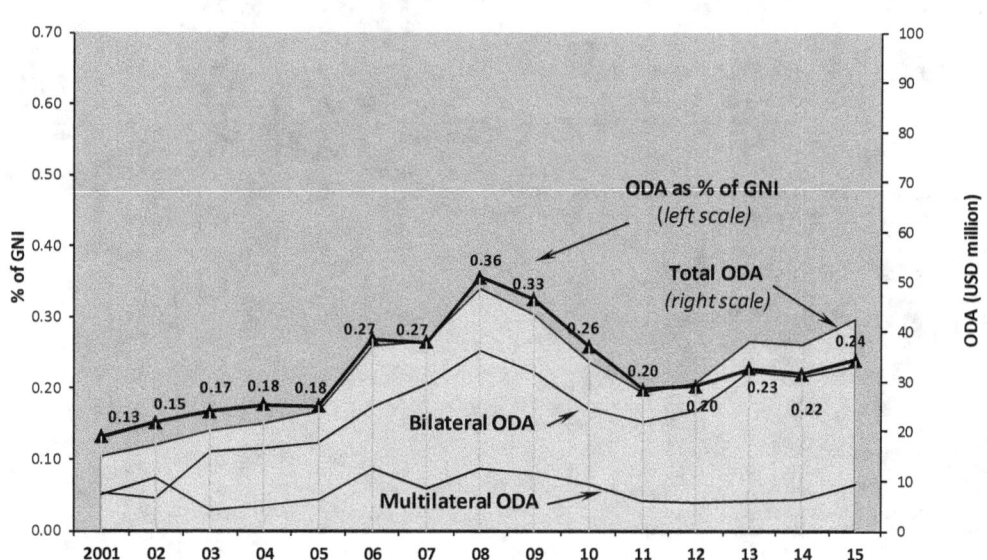

ODA net disbursements
At constant 2014 prices and exchange rates and as a share of GNI

Annex A: OECD/DAC standard suite of tables

Table A.2 ODA by main categories

Disbursements

Iceland	Constant 2014 USD million					Per cent share of gross disbursements					Total DAC 2015%
	2011	2012	2013	2014	2015	2011	2012	2013	2014	2015	
Gross Bilateral ODA	22	24	32	31	33	78	81	84	83	78	74
Budget support	-	-	-	-	-	-	-	-	-	-	2
of which: General budget support	-	-	-	-	-	-	-	-	-	-	1
Core contributions & pooled prog.& funds	10	9	11	11	12	35	30	29	29	28	14
of which: Core support to national NGOs	1	0	0	0	0	4	0	0	0	0	2
Core support to international NGOs	0	0	0	0	0	1	0	0	0	0	1
Core support to PPPs	-	-	-	-	-	-	-	-	-	-	0
Project-type interventions	8	10	15	12	11	28	35	39	32	26	39
of which: Investment projects	-	-	-	-	-	-	-	-	-	-	14
Experts and other technical assistance	2	2	3	3	2	6	8	9	8	5	4
Scholarships and student costs in donor countries	-	-	-	-	-	-	-	-	-	-	2
of which: Imputed student costs	-	-	-	-	-	-	-	-	-	-	1
Debt relief grants	0	-	-	-	-	1	-	-	-	-	0
Administrative costs	2	2	2	2	3	7	7	6	7	6	4
Other in-donor expenditures	0	0	1	3	5	1	1	2	8	13	9
of which: refugees in donor countries	0	0	0	3	5	1	1	1	7	12	
Gross Multilateral ODA	6	6	6	6	9	22	19	16	17	22	26
UN agencies	3	3	3	3	3	12	9	8	7	7	4
EU institutions	-	-	-	-	-	-	-	-	-	-	8
World Bank group	2	2	2	3	5	8	7	5	8	13	6
Regional development banks	-	-	-	-	-	-	-	-	-	-	2
Other multilateral	1	1	1	1	1	2	3	3	2	3	5
Total gross ODA	28	30	38	37	42	100	100	100	100	100	100
of which: Gross ODA loans	-	-	-	-	-	-	-	-	-	-	14
Bilateral	-	-	-	-	-	-	-	-	-	-	13
Multilateral	-	-	-	-	-	-	-	-	-	-	1
Repayments and debt cancellation	-	-	-	-	-						
Total net ODA	28	30	38	37	42						
For reference:											
Free standing technical co-operation	-	-	2	3	3						
Net debt relief	-	0	-	-	-						

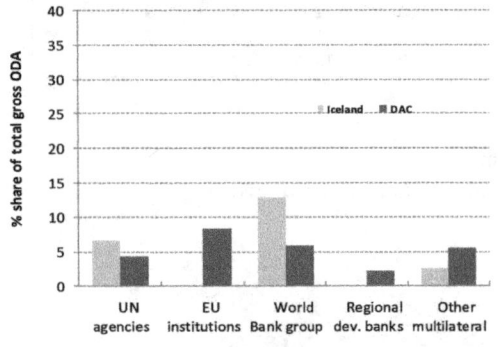

ODA flows to multilateral agencies, 2015

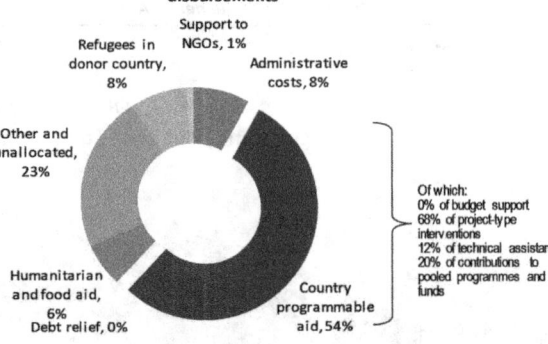

Composition of bilateral ODA, 2014, gross bilateral disbursements

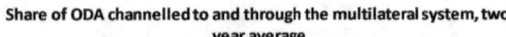

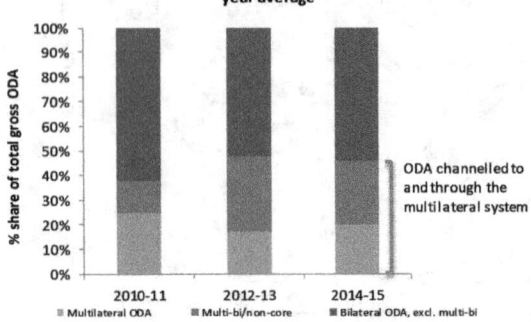

Share of ODA channelled to and through the multilateral system, two year average

Annex A: OECD/DAC standard suite of tables

Table A.3 Bilateral ODA allocable by region and income group

Gross disbursements

Iceland	Constant 2014 USD million					% share					Total DAC
	2011	2012	2013	2014	2015	2011	2012	2013	2014	2015	2015%
Africa	11	11	17	15	14	74	75	78	80	74	41
Sub-Saharan Africa	11	11	17	15	14	73	75	78	80	74	35
North Africa	0	-	-	-	-	1	-	-	-	-	4
Asia	1	1	1	1	1	10	7	7	4	5	31
South and Central Asia	1	1	1	1	1	10	7	5	4	5	19
Far East	-	-	0	-	0	-	-	2	-	0	12
America	1	1	0	-	-	6	7	1	-	-	10
North and Central America	1	1	0	-	-	6	5	1	-	-	4
South America	-	0	0	-	-	-	2	1	-	-	5
Middle East	1	2	3	2	3	6	10	12	13	17	10
Oceania	-	-	-	-	-	-	-	-	-	-	2
Europe	1	0	0	1	1	4	1	2	4	4	5
Total bilateral allocable by region	15	15	21	19	19	100	100	100	100	100	100
Least developed	11	12	16	13	14	81	82	82	81	78	40
Other low-income	-	0	-	-	-	-	2	-	-	-	4
Lower middle-income	2	2	3	3	2	13	16	17	17	13	35
Upper middle-income	1	0	0	0	2	6	0	1	2	9	21
More advanced developing countries	-	-	-	-	-	-	-	-	-	-	-
Total bilateral allocable by income	13	14	19	16	18	100	100	100	100	100	100
For reference:											
Total bilateral	22	24	32	31	33	*100*	*100*	*100*	*100*	*100*	*100*
of which: Unallocated by region	7	9	11	12	14	32	37	33	40	43	32
of which: Unallocated by income	9	10	13	15	15	39	42	40	48	47	40

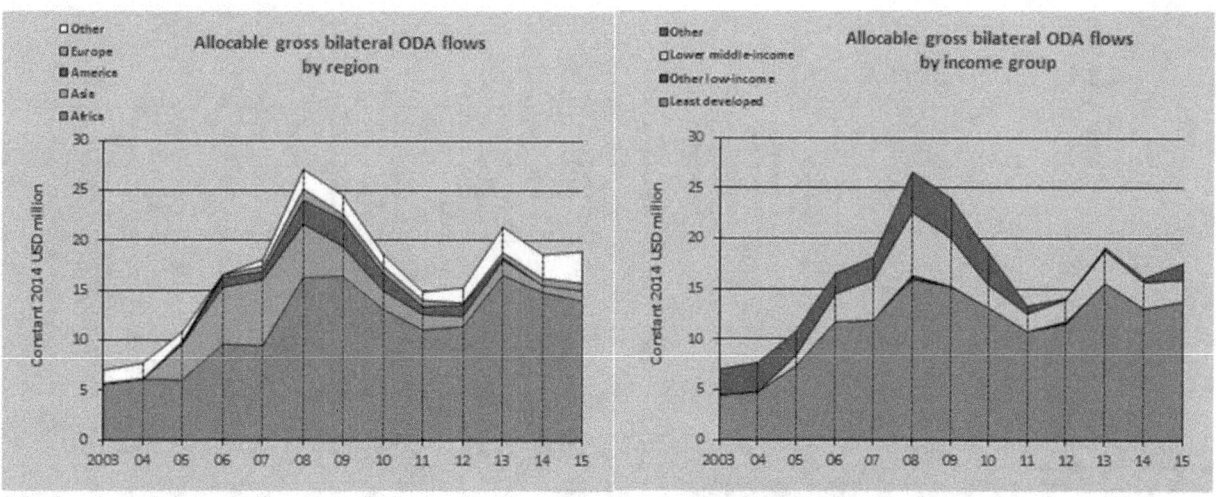

1. Each region includes regional amounts which cannot be allocated by sub-region. The sum of the sub-regional amounts may therefore fall short of the regional total.

Annex A: OECD/DAC standard suite of tables

Table A.4 Main recipients of bilateral ODA

Iceland	2004-08 average			Memo: DAC countries' average %	Slovenia	2009-13 average			Memo: DAC countries' average %		2014-15 average (Gross disbursements)			Memo: DAC countries' average %
	Current USD million	Constant 2014 USD mln	% share			Current USD million	Constant 2014 USD mln	% share			Current USD million	Constant 2014 USD mln	% share	
Malawi	3.5	3.2	13		Malawi	3.5	4.0	15		Malawi	4.9	5.1	16	
Afghanistan	2.9	2.6	11		Uganda	3.3	3.8	14		Uganda	3.4	3.5	11	
Mozambique	2.4	2.2	9		Mozambique	2.2	2.5	10		Mozambique	3.0	3.1	10	
Uganda	2.2	2.0	8		West Bank and Gaza Strip	1.1	1.3	5		West Bank and Gaza Strip	1.3	1.3	4	
Sri Lanka	1.9	1.6	7		Afghanistan	1.1	1.3	5		Syrian Arab Republic	0.8	0.8	3	
Top 5 recipients	12.9	11.6	47	36	**Top 5 recipients**	11.4	13.0	49	26	**Top 5 recipients**	13.4	13.8	43	22
Namibia	1.8	1.6	6		Namibia	1.0	1.2	4		Afghanistan	0.7	0.7	2	
Nicaragua	0.9	0.8	3		Nicaragua	0.7	0.8	3		Lebanon	0.6	0.6	2	
Iraq	0.6	0.6	2		Guinea-Bissau	0.3	0.4	1		Ethiopia	0.4	0.4	1	
West Bank and Gaza Strip	0.4	0.3	1		Ethiopia	0.2	0.3	1		Ukraine	0.3	0.3	1	
Bosnia and Herzegovina	0.2	0.2	1		Haiti	0.2	0.2	1		Belarus	0.2	0.2	1	
Top 10 recipients	16.8	15.1	61	48	**Top 10 recipients**	13.8	16.0	59	37	**Top 10 recipients**	15.5	16.0	50	33
Lebanon	0.2	0.2	1		Syrian Arab Republic	0.2	0.2	1		Nepal	0.2	0.2	0	
Sudan	0.2	0.2	1		Sri Lanka	0.2	0.2	1		Sierra Leone	0.1	0.1	0	
Serbia	0.1	0.1	1		Bosnia and Herzegovina	0.1	0.2	1		Guinea-Bissau	0.1	0.1	0	
Liberia	0.1	0.1	0		Liberia	0.1	0.1	0		Serbia	0.1	0.1	0	
Kenya	0.1	0.1	0		Somalia	0.1	0.1	0		Somalia	0.1	0.1	0	
Top 15 recipients	17.4	15.8	63	57	**Top 15 recipients**	14.6	16.8	62	44	**Top 15 recipients**	16.0	16.5	52	41
Guinea-Bissau	0.1	0.1	0		Sudan	0.1	0.1	0		South Africa	0.1	0.1	0	
Former Yugoslav Republic of Macedonia	0.0	0.0	0		Pakistan	0.1	0.1	0		Central African Republic	0.1	0.1	0	
India	0.0	0.0	0		Philippines	0.1	0.1	0		South Sudan	0.1	0.1	0	
South Africa	0.0	0.0	0		Jordan	0.1	0.1	0		Yemen	0.0	0.0	0	
Nepal	0.0	0.0	0		Kenya	0.1	0.1	0		Namibia	0.0	0.0	0	
Top 20 recipients	17.6	15.9	64	63	**Top 20 recipients**	15.0	17.3	64	49	**Top 20 recipients**	16.2	16.8	52	47
Total (20 recipients)	17.6	15.9	64		**Total (38 recipients)**	15.4	17.8	66		**Total (24 recipients)**	16.3	16.8	53	
Unallocated	9.9	9.0	36	24	Unallocated	8.0	9.0	34	33	Unallocated	14.7	15.2	47	40
Total bilateral gross	27.5	24.9	100	100	**Total bilateral gross**	23.3	26.8	100	100	**Total bilateral gross**	31.0	32.0	100	100

Annex A: OECD/DAC standard suite of tables

Table A.5 Bilateral ODA by major purposes
at constant prices and exchange rates

Commitments - Two-year average

Iceland	2013-14 average		2014-15 average		2014-15
	2014 USD million	%	2014 USD million	%	%
Social infrastructure & services	13	46	14	44	36
Education	3	10	2	6	7
of which: basic education	2	8	2	6	2
Health	3	10	2	6	5
of which: basic health	3	9	2	6	4
Population & reproductive health	0	1	0	0	7
Water supply & sanitation	1	3	2	7	4
Government & civil society	3	12	4	11	11
of which: Conflict, peace & security	1	3	1	3	2
Other social infrastructure & services	3	10	4	13	2
Economic infrastructure & services	4	15	4	12	19
Transport & storage	-	-	-	-	7
Communications	-	-	-	-	0
Energy	4	15	4	12	8
Banking & financial services	0	0	0	0	2
Business & other services	-	-	-	-	1
Production sectors	6	23	4	14	7
Agriculture, forestry & fishing	6	22	4	14	5
Industry, mining & construction	0	0	-	-	1
Trade & tourism	-	-	-	-	1
Multisector	1	2	0	1	10
Commodity and programme aid	-	-	-	-	2
Action relating to debt	-	-	-	-	0
Humanitarian aid	1	5	3	9	12
Administrative costs of donors	2	8	3	8	6
Refugees in donor countries	0	1	4	12	8
Total bilateral allocable	**28**	**100**	**32**	**100**	**100**
For reference:					
Total bilateral	28	83	32	80	73
of which: Unallocated	0	1	0	1	1
Total multilateral	6	17	8	20	27
Total ODA	34	100	40	100	100

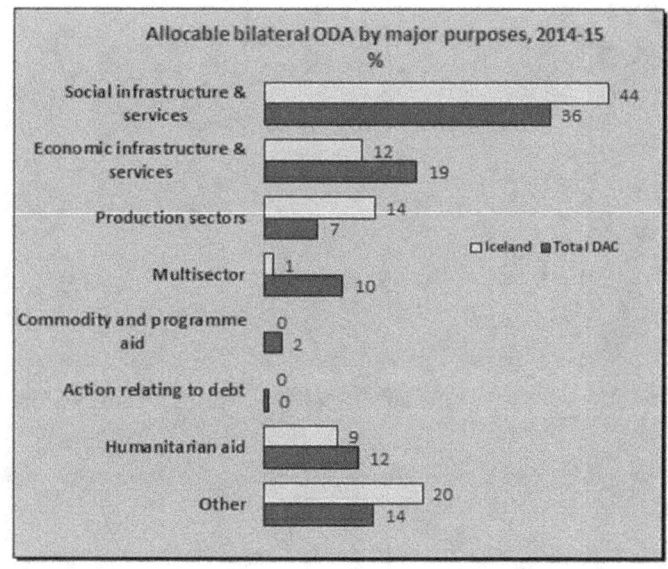

Annex A: OECD/DAC standard suite of tables

Table A.6 Comparative aid performance

	Official development assistance			Net disbursements				Grant element of ODA commitments	Commitments Untied aid % of bilateral commitments
	2015		2009-10 to 2014-15 Average annual % change in real terms	Share of multilateral aid 2015				2015	Year
				% of ODA		% of GNI			
	USD million	% of GNI		(b)	(c)	(b)	(c)	% (a)	(d)
Australia	3 494	0.29	2.7	21.2		0.06		99.9	100.0
Austria	1 324	0.35	2.5	40.9	20.7	0.14	0.07	100.0	36.4
Belgium	1 905	0.42	-4.3	41.6	17.3	0.17	0.07	99.8	96.7
Canada	4 277	0.28	-1.4	30.5		0.09		97.3	98.5
Czech Republic	199	0.12	1.0	64.8	11.2	0.08	0.01	100.0	44.3
Denmark	2 566	0.85	0.3	26.7	17.4	0.23	0.15	100.0	100.0
Finland	1 288	0.55	2.3	45.8	32.5	0.25	0.18	100.0	92.6
France	9 039	0.37	-3.9	42.9	21.5	0.16	0.08	79.6	95.6
Germany	17 940	0.52	7.5	21.3	7.6	0.11	0.04	86.6	84.0
Greece	239	0.12	-12.5	69.9	3.7	0.09	0.00	100.0	14.5
Iceland	40	0.24	0.7	22.1		0.05		100.0	100.0
Ireland	718	0.32	-2.8	40.5	20.8	0.13	0.07	100.0	100.0
Italy	4 004	0.22	6.3	54.3	18.7	0.12	0.04	99.6	95.1
Japan	9 203	0.21	3.0	33.2		0.07		87.5	74.6
Korea	1 915	0.14	10.0	20.1		0.03		95.3	50.2
Luxembourg	363	0.95	-1.5	27.6	19.8	0.26	0.19	100.0	98.8
Netherlands	5 726	0.75	-1.0	27.3	17.8	0.20	0.13	100.0	92.7
New Zealand	442	0.27	3.1	18.9		0.05		100.0	84.7
Norway	4 278	1.05	1.9	22.7		0.24		100.0	100.0
Poland	441	0.10	4.4	77.3	10.2	0.07	0.01	98.6	33.6
Portugal	308	0.16	-7.5	52.6	5.6	0.08	0.01	93.7	49.0
Slovak Republic	85	0.10	4.1	79.7	17.5	0.08	0.02	100.0	47.5
Slovenia	63	0.15	1.1	60.3	11.0	0.09	0.02	100.0	12.4
Spain	1 397	0.12	-22.0	74.6	9.7	0.09	0.01	100.0	80.8
Sweden	7 089	1.40	7.4	31.9	26.1	0.45	0.37	100.0	86.8
Switzerland	3 562	0.52	6.5	22.5		0.12		100.0	94.6
United Kingdom	18 545	0.70	6.8	36.9	25.9	0.26	0.18	100.0	100.0
United States	30 986	0.17	0.2	14.0		0.02		100.0	55.5
Total DAC	131 433	0.30	1.6	28.3		0.08		94.4	78.1
Memo: Average country effort		0.41							

Notes:
a. Excluding debt reorganisation.
b. Including EU institutions.
c. Excluding EU institutions.
d. Excluding administrative costs and in-donor refugee costs.
.. Data not available.

Annex A: OECD/DAC standard suite of tables

Table A.7 Comparative aid performance to LDCs

	Net disbursements						Commitments		
	Bilateral ODA to LDCs 2015			Total ODA to LDCs (Bilateral and through multilateral agencies) 2015			Grant element of bilateral ODA commitments[a] to LDCs (two alternative norms)		
							Annually for all LDCs Norm: 90%		3-year average for each LDC Norm: 86%
	USD million	% bilateral ODA	% of GNI	USD million	% total ODA	% of GNI	2014	2015	2013-2015
Australia	679	24.7	0.06	931	26.6	0.08	100.0	100.0	c
Austria	41	5.3	0.01	222	16.8	0.06	100.0	100.0	c
Belgium	377	33.9	0.08	610	32.0	0.13	99.6	99.3	n
Canada	998	33.6	0.07	1 561	36.5	0.10	100.0	100.0	c
Czech Republic	11	16.4	0.01	41	20.7	0.02	100.0	100.0	c
Denmark	384	20.4	0.13	610	23.8	0.20	100.0	100.0	c
Finland	236	33.8	0.10	429	33.3	0.18	100.0	100.0	c
France	1 090	21.1	0.04	2 378	26.3	0.10	82.2	79.8	n
Germany	1 603	11.4	0.05	2 596	14.5	0.08	98.7	98.5	c
Greece	1	1.6	0.00	38	16.0	0.02	100.0	100.0	c
Iceland	13	41.6	0.08	16	40.8	0.10	100.0	100.0	c
Ireland	257	60.1	0.11	345	48.0	0.15	100.0	100.0	c
Italy	280	15.3	0.02	870	21.7	0.05	99.1	98.9	c
Japan	2 480	40.3	0.06	3 659	39.8	0.08	93.2	91.3	c
Korea	580	37.9	0.04	728	38.0	0.05	94.4	95.0	c
Luxembourg	121	46.2	0.32	154	42.4	0.40	100.0	100.0	c
Netherlands	465	11.2	0.06	1 036	18.1	0.14	100.0	100.0	c
New Zealand	113	31.7	0.07	138	31.3	0.08	100.0	100.0	c
Norway	729	22.1	0.18	1 098	25.7	0.27	100.0	100.0	c
Poland	44	44.2	0.01	125	28.4	0.03	78.8	83.9	n
Portugal	53	36.3	0.03	90	29.3	0.05	87.9	92.0	n
Slovak Republic	1	5.4	0.00	19	21.8	0.02	100.0	100.0	c
Slovenia	0	1.6	0.00	10	15.1	0.02	100.0	100.0	c
Spain	81	22.9	0.01	314	22.5	0.03	100.0	100.0	c
Sweden	847	17.6	0.17	1 473	20.8	0.29	100.0	100.0	c
Switzerland	618	22.4	0.09	928	26.1	0.14	100.0	100.0	c
United Kingdom	3 815	32.6	0.14	6 117	33.0	0.23	100.0	100.0	c
United States	9 122	34.2	0.05	10 737	34.7	0.06	100.0	100.0	c
Total DAC	25 041	26.6	0.06	37 274	28.4	0.09	97.6	96.9	..

Notes:
a. Excluding debt reorganisation. Equities are treated as having 100% grant element, but are not treated as loans.
b. c = compliance, n = non compliance.
.. Data not available.

Annex A: OECD/DAC standard suite of tables

Figure A.1 Net ODA from DAC countries in 2015

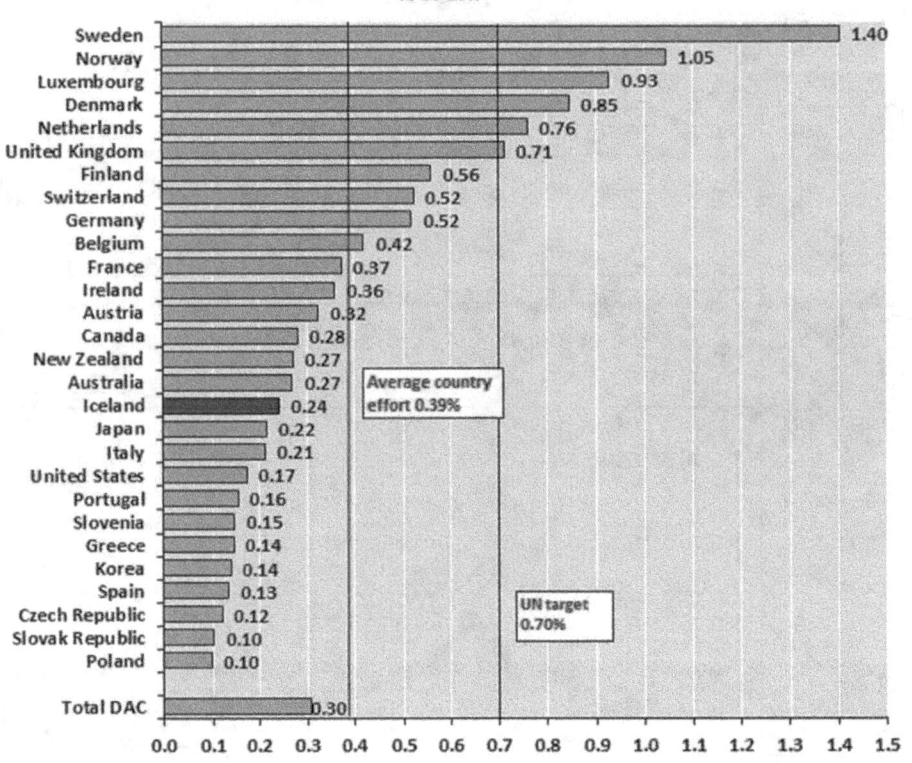

Annex B: Organisational structure

Figure B.1 Organigram of the Ministry for Foreign Affairs

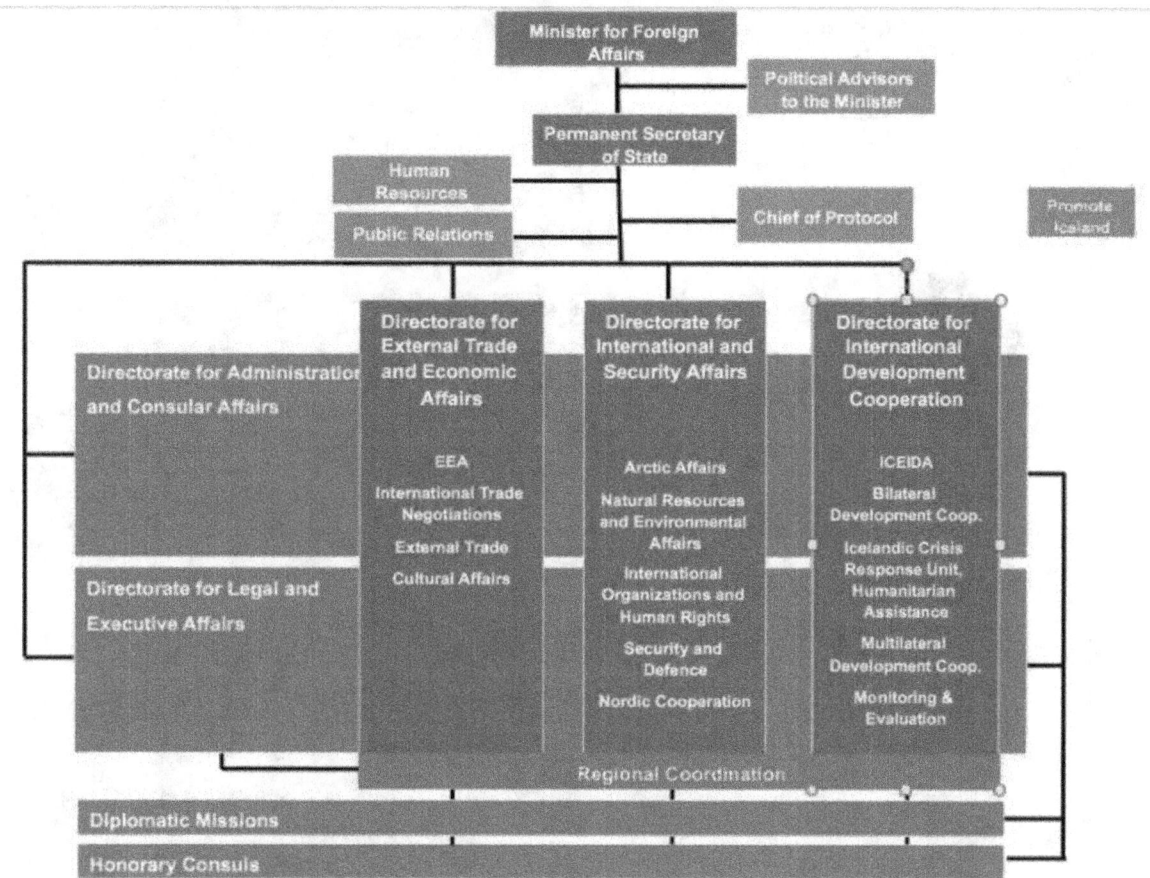

Source: provided by Ministry for Foreign Affairs of Iceland (2016)

Annex B: Organisational structure

Figure B.2. Iceland's Team on International Development Co-operation

ICELAND'S TEAM ON INTERNATIONAL DEVELOPMENT COOPERATION (þSS)

þSS Director General — Secretary

Consultation Team

Cross cutting/other projects in the field of development cooperation
- Regional Cooperation in the field of Climate Change
- The UNU in Iceland - setup of a new Institution
- Private Sector Participation in Developing Cooperation
- Cooperation with the OECD/DAC
- Focus Area Hub: Energy

(Minister Counsellor, Project Manager, Consultant)

Bilateral Cooperation
- Operations in bilateral partner countries: Malawi, Mozambique and Uganda
- Earmarked contributions to multilateral organisations
- Cooperation with NGOs
- Hub for UNU Training Programmes in Iceland

Focus Area Hub:
- Education
- Health
- Fisheries
- Land Restoration

(Director, adviser)

Multilateral Cooperation
- Cooperation with the UN, World Bank and other multilateral banks and entities
- Core Contributions to multilateral organisations
- International Cooperation and advocacy: Nordic Plus, Global Partnership for Effective Development Cooperation, SDGs, Financing for Development
- Committee on International Development Cooperation

Focus Area Hub:
- Gender Equality
- Environment

(Director, 2 advisers)

Humanitarian Assistance
- ICRU, contributions and seconded personnel
- Humanitarian assistance
- Election Observation

Focus Area Hub:
- UNSCR 1325

(Director, adviser)

Evaluation and Results
- Evaluations of projects, programmes, institutions and policies
- Results Report - Iceland's Policy for International Development Cooperation
- Results Report - Policies for gender equality and the environment

(Director, adviser)

Iceland's Embassies in Malawi, Mozambique and Uganda
(Heads of Missions, Programme Managers, locally hired employees)

Committee on International Development Cooperation

RPS Development Finance (Director, adviser)

LoS Publication and PR for International Development Cooperation (Adviser)

LoS Archiving for International Development Cooperation (Adviser)

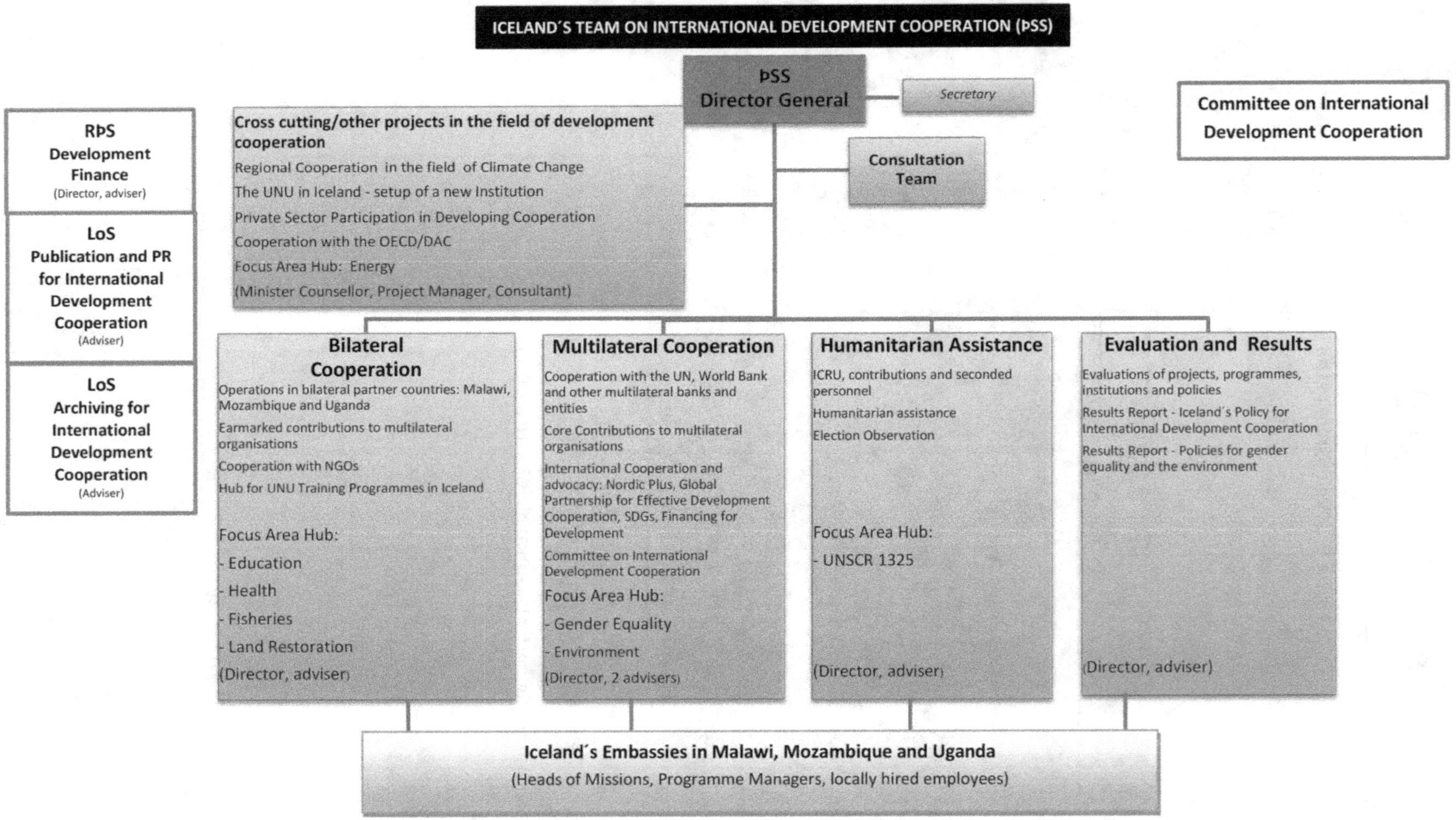

Source: provided by Ministry for Foreign Affairs of Iceland (2016)

Annex C: Perspectives from Malawi, Mozambique and Uganda on Icelandic development co-operation

Iceland has a long tradition of bilateral development co-operation, with a field presence in its partner countries. To understand how Iceland delivers its development co-operation in its key partner countries, the peer review team held meetings in Reykjavik with the Icelandic chargés d'affaires based in Malawi, Mozambique and Uganda, as well as with officials from the Ministry for Foreign Affairs and a Chief District Health Officer from the Mangochi District in Malawi. In addition, the team also met and organised phone interviews with partner country stakeholders to deepen the field perspective.

Iceland's policies, strategies and aid allocations to Malawi, Mozambique and Uganda

Iceland's support to its partner countries builds on a long history of co-operation

Iceland has been providing official development assistance (ODA) to a range of partners since 1981. The economic and financial crisis in 2008 led to a reduction in the number of Iceland's partner countries. It withdrew from Nicaragua and Sri Lanka in 2009 and from Namibia in 2010 in order to concentrate its operations in Malawi, Mozambique and Uganda. In 2014, Iceland spent 44% of its bilateral ODA in these three countries. Its co-operation focuses on supporting social infrastructure.

Malawi is Iceland's largest recipient of bilateral assistance, receiving on average USD 4.5 million annually between 2011 and 2015 (Figure C.1). Iceland was the 11th largest DAC donor in Malawi during that period, providing the equivalent of 0.65% of Malawi's total net official development assistance (ODA). Iceland concentrates all of its aid in Mangochi district (one of the poorest districts in the country), where it has been implementing projects since 1989. The current Malawi country strategy paper and Mangochi Basic Services Programme (2012-16) focus on social infrastructure sectors (education, maternal health, water and sanitation). In addition, Iceland provides expertise and builds the capacity of local stakeholders operating in these sectors, including district authorities. Iceland's activities include a cross-sectoral focus on the empowerment of women and young people. Iceland also supported humanitarian efforts in Malawi during the food crises of 2012-13 and 2015.

Iceland takes a similar programmatic approach in its co-operation with Uganda, where it has operated since 2000. It disbursed on average USD 3.7 million annually to Uganda between 2011 and 2015 (Figure C.1). Iceland is Uganda's 19th largest DAC donor, providing the equivalent of 0.31% of Uganda's total net ODA over this four-year period. Iceland works in the Kalangala and Buikwe districts. In Buikwe, it implements a multi-sector programme, involving education, water and sanitation. Iceland is considering the possibility of expanding its activities in Buikwe to the fisheries and health sectors (Government of Iceland, 2013). In Kalangala, the programme targets the fisheries,

Annex C: Perspectives from Malawi, Mozambique and Uganda on Icelandic development co-operation

health and tourism sectors. However, after a mid-term review of its programme, Iceland decided to shift allocations from tourism to education in Kalangala. It is noteworthy that Iceland's district programmes are highly focused on cross-district learning.

Figure C.1 Icelandic ODA disbursements to Malawi, Mozambique and Uganda 2011-14

Gross disbursements, USD million, 2014 constant prices

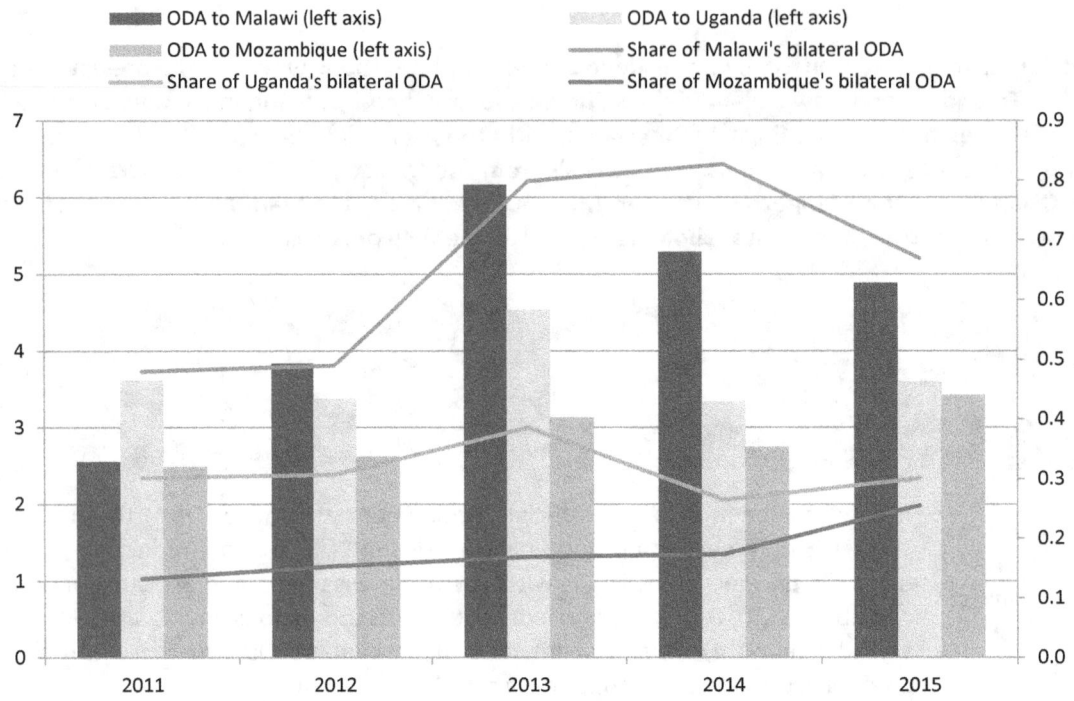

Source: OECD (2017), "Geographical distribution of financial flows: flows to developing countries", OECD International Development Statistics (database), http://dx.doi.org/10.1787/data-00566-en (accessed 16 January 2017).

Mozambique is Iceland's third largest bilateral partner country, with co-operation dating back to 1995. Iceland disbursed on average USD 2.9 million to Mozambique between 2011 and 2015 (Figure C.1). Iceland is the 22nd largest DAC donor in Mozambique, where it provided the equivalent of 0.18% of Mozambique's total net ODA over the period. Iceland initially worked in the adult education sector in the Inhambane province and in the fisheries sector in the Zambezia province. However, key evaluations have found that Iceland's approach in Mozambique has not been as successful as in Malawi or Uganda (e.g. failure of the adult literacy and life skills project; Government of Iceland, 2013). Given that Iceland is one of the smallest DAC donors in Mozambique, it should consider how to increase the impact of its presence in Mozambique. One way would be to continue working in partnership with other donors, as Iceland already does through a fisheries project with Norway. Another approach would be to transfer more bilateral funding through multilateral channels. Iceland is also doing this with the UNICEF Water, Sanitation and Hygiene programme – in the form of earmarked contributions.

Annex C: Perspectives from Malawi, Mozambique and Uganda on Icelandic development co-operation

Iceland makes the most of bilateral and multilateral synergies

Iceland is able to forge close links between its bilateral and key multilateral development co-operation activities, in particular in its three priority partner countries. Iceland's preferred multilateral partners in all three countries are the World Food Programme, UNICEF and UN Women. In designing its programmes, Iceland provides earmarked contributions to these multilateral organisations and draws on their expertise. For example, in Uganda, Iceland sought expertise from UN Women when preparing its programme for Buikwe District; in Mozambique, Iceland funds (and monitors) a project on water and sanitation implemented by UNICEF.

Iceland mainly prefers to work with multilateral agencies and pooled funds to support emergency situations (Chapter 7). For example, Iceland channelled its emergency aid through multilateral organisations in Malawi, such as the World Food Programme which delivered food after the 2012-13 drought and the 2015 floods. Iceland also piloted a project to introduce home-grown school meals in Malawi, building synergies with Iceland's education and health sectoral priorities in the country.

Iceland draws on its bilateral experience and achievements to enhance its multilateral efforts. This, in turn, strengthens its bilateral efforts. Such feedback loops across delivery channels ensure that Iceland adds value to its partner countries by filling gaps in expertise and seeking complementarities with multilateral organisations to deliver quality aid. However, Iceland could further explore how to build synergies with its other priority multilateral organisations, in particular the United Nations University (UNU), which could help it provide training directly in its partner countries. The University's Geothermal Programme, in fact, has been providing such training in several countries and could share this experience with the other UNU programmes.

Iceland's shift from projects to programmes is reflected in its planning and programming processes

In general terms, Iceland has transitioned from (primarily) working with national and district authorities to support fishing communities, to providing the social infrastructure (health, education, water and sanitation) that underpin these communities in selected, isolated districts. It has more recently moved away from providing basic social services through projects to a more programmatic approach whereby it transfers funds and devolves responsibility to district administration. This district-level approach aims to build capacity, fill gaps and implement district-driven solutions.

This switch to using local programming and results frameworks has been coupled with changes in Iceland's own programming processes, which have become more detailed, evidence-based and rigorous. This new programmatic approach is outlined in medium-term country strategy papers aligned with the national development co-operation strategy and then cascade into general basic social infrastructure programmes for the districts. These, in turn, lead to specific sectoral plans for these districts. All these documents are discussed and agreed with district councils and relevant ministries at national level, and disbursements are in line with country paper financial plans.

Iceland also relies on mid-term reviews of its country programmes to learn from on-going challenges and strengths. End of programme evaluations are also scheduled during the programming phase, and provide information that can improve programme quality and results. However, these evaluations could reflect more deeply on how Iceland can ensure that the recurrent transaction costs from district administration that were occasionally met by ICEIDA do not undermine the achievement of planned programme results.

Annex C: Perspectives from Malawi, Mozambique and Uganda on Icelandic development co-operation

Iceland takes a holistic approach to community development

Fisheries, an area where Iceland possesses both expertise and experience, have been at the core of Iceland's bilateral development efforts since its inception. Initially, Iceland implemented projects in this sector in most of its partner countries. However, Iceland's focus has gradually broadened to improve living conditions in the districts it operates, thereby also providing a more holistic frame for its development aims.

Iceland selects partner countries on the basis of their development needs, their relatively small population size, stable governance that allows for long-term planning, and other logistical and practical criteria, including Iceland's own track record in these countries (Chapter 2). These criteria indicate Iceland's potential impact on poverty and its contribution to fostering sustainable development.

Iceland is making efforts in Malawi and, especially, in Uganda to analyse revenue options and plans to increase local resource mobilisation, including from central government, to promote self-sufficiency and sustainability. In the future, to ensure the sustainability of its investments, Iceland needs to find ways to encourage national governments to take over the funding of these activities in line with national priorities. According to interviewees met in Reykjavik, the funding that district councils agree with the national government often does not trickle-down to the districts, compromising the sustainability of Icelandic investments.

Drawing on its experience in the social sector at district level, Iceland could apply a fragility lens to its operation in Malawi and Uganda, to promote a government buy-in and increase both the resilience of vulnerable populations and the sustainability of its development investments.

Organisation and management

Iceland's foreign missions are central to its bilateral aid delivery model

Iceland's former development agency, ICEIDA, was responsible for implementing bilateral development co-operation in its partner countries, while the Ministry for Foreign Affairs could complement these activities with support to multilateral organisations working in-country. As a result of the merger of ICEIDA with the ministry in 2016, Iceland has improved efficiencies. The ministry now centralises all development co-operation activities, from planning to implementation and evaluation, which has streamlined processes and reduced transaction costs.

Iceland's Ambassador to Malawi, Mozambique and Uganda also acts as Head of the Development Co-operation Directorate in the Ministry for Foreign Affairs. Though Iceland's embassies are based in capitals, in Malawi, Mozambique and Uganda there are also offices in the district capitals. The embassies now have a single development co-operation mandate, and receive directions from only one institution at headquarters. Iceland's field missions co-ordinate with partner country governments, local district governments, key stakeholders and other donors. Local stakeholder participation is emphasised throughout the programme implementation cycle to ensure ownership, achieve better and more efficient results and minimise risks.

However, due to the financial crisis and the shift to programme-based activities, the total number of staff working in the field has decreased. This reduction has largely concerned local staff, although part of this fall was also due to the programmatic shift in Iceland's local operations.

Annex C: Perspectives from Malawi, Mozambique and Uganda on Icelandic development co-operation

Greater attention needs to be given to environmental mainstreaming and evaluation in the programme design phase

Programmes are prepared in collaboration with governments and other stakeholders in partner countries, in line with respective country strategy papers and district-level plans – and in line with Iceland's Quality Manual and Rules of Procedure. While gender and the environment are routinely mainstreamed into all of Iceland's operations, practical design tools are needed for implementing these actions in the field. Iceland could rely on the tools developed by other bilateral and multilateral donors and integrate these into its district and sectoral programmes.

Iceland also needs to improve the timeliness of its mid-term evaluations. Although mid-term and end-of-term evaluations are scheduled during the programme preparation phase, with on-going monitoring, mid-term evaluations for its partner countries were not conducted when originally planned. As a result there is little evidence available to influence shifts in context and to feed into programme updates.

Partnerships, results and accountability

Iceland works efficiently with district systems

Iceland is commended for making good use of district systems in its partner countries, following its own financial risk management assessments. For example, in Malawi's Mangochi District, Iceland uses existing district systems for financial management, financial reporting and public procurement. Iceland also invests in developing district-level capacities to manage and track its aid. In assessing the risks and benefits associated with using local systems, Iceland found that the Mangochi district systems could supply quality data and had the required capacity for Iceland's monitoring purposes.

The Mangochi District Council is responsible for the planning, tendering and financial administration of the activities and projects defined in Iceland's programme documents for Malawi. Periodic spot checks by Iceland's local staff and the Ministry for Foreign Affairs ensure financial probity and that Iceland's funds are managed to match Icelandic standards. The programme also follows Malawian law, regulations and procedures for public procurement.[1] When challenges occur or inefficiencies are detected, Iceland engages in dialogue with all stakeholders involved. This encourages ownership by the District Council and local stakeholders. Evidence in the mid-term review of the Malawi programme reveals that this approach is serving Iceland and its partners well (Mkamanga, 2014).

Iceland co-ordinates well with other donors but could work more with NGOs

Iceland is actively involved in donor co-ordination groups in its three partner countries, which helps it spread risk, build synergies, enhance its knowledge of partner country needs and opportunities, and ultimately add value to its partnerships. For example, Iceland regularly chairs the Heads of Cooperation Group in Malawi, where discussions centre on areas of shared interest, such as a common anti-corruption stance or developing a harmonised system of daily allowances. Similar co-ordination can also be observed in Uganda and Mozambique, as well as in its regional project on geothermal energy. Iceland makes good use of the findings from such co-ordination fora to feed into planning and programming, in particular with Nordic countries.

Iceland would do well to extend this national-level co-ordination to disaster risk and resilience activities. In addition, it could make greater use of its collaboration with non-government organisations (NGOs) – both Icelandic and local organisations – operating

Annex C: Perspectives from Malawi, Mozambique and Uganda on Icelandic development co-operation

	in its partner countries to learn from their experience and improve the communication of development results to the Icelandic public.
Iceland is reconsidering its approach to results management	Consultations with partners during programme preparation ensure that Iceland's strategic priorities and expected results are aligned with those of their partner countries. Iceland uses baseline studies and local results indicators in its priority countries, and adds indicators where gaps exist, in consultation with district partners.
	External evaluations of completed projects suggest that Iceland's development aid has been well spent. For example, the mid-term evaluation of a water and sanitation project in Malawi found significant improvements in the living conditions and health of the target population (Mkamanga, 2014). A comprehensive evaluation of the former co-operation between Iceland and Namibia in fisheries also confirmed that important and lasting results had been achieved. Iceland is currently considering how its outcomes-based approach to results management can help it communicate progress in a way that is relevant to the Sustainable Development Goals. This is particularly challenging given that work on measuring results at sub-national levels is in its very early stages (Chapter 6). In the meantime, Iceland could extend its work on communicating district-level results to increase public understanding of its aid programme. For example, Iceland's contribution of USD 2 million a year to Malawi's health sector is unlikely to influence maternal death rates in any significant way at the national level. However, this spending on the health programme in Mangochi district has provided 20 000 women with better health services and access to drinking water (OECD, 2016). This type of framework is much more meaningful to Iceland and its stakeholders.

Annex C: Perspectives from Malawi, Mozambique and Uganda on Icelandic development co-operation

Notes

1. Iceland also delegates responsibilities to other stakeholders at district level, for example to water point committees which manage and maintain water pumps financed or installed in the past with Icelandic aid.

Annex C: Perspectives from Malawi, Mozambique and Uganda on Icelandic development co-operation

Bibliography

Government sources

Government of Iceland (2016), *Buikwe-ICEIDA Development Partnership: Education Development in Fishing Communities 2016-19*, Reykjavik: Government of Iceland.

Government of Iceland (2016), "OECD DAC peer review of Iceland: memorandum", Government of Iceland, Reykjavik.

Government of Iceland (2013), *Support to the Fisheries Sector of Mozambique 2013-2017 Programme Document Common Fund*, Government of Iceland, Reykjavik, www.iceida.is/media/verkefnagagnabanki/Support-to-the-Fisheries-Sector-of-Mozambique-2013-2017---Programme-Document-Common-Fund.pdf.

Government of Iceland (2012), *Mangochi Basic Services Programme 2012-2016*, Government of Iceland, Reykjavik.

ICEIDA (2014), *Uganda Country Strategy Paper 2014-2017*, Icelandic International Development Agency, Reykjavik, www.iceida.is/media/pdf/Uganda-CSP-2014-2017.pdf.

ICEIDA (2012), *Malawi Country Strategy Paper 2012-2016*, Icelandic International Development Agency, Reykjavik, www.iceida.is/media/pdf/Malawi_CSP_2012-2016.pdf.

MFA (2016), *Evaluation Policy for Iceland's Development Cooperation*, Ministry for Foreign Affairs, Reykjavik.

Other sources

Mkamanga, G. (2014), "Mangochi Basic Services Programme 2012-2016: mid-term evaluation", Final report, Icelandic International Development Agency, Reykjavik, www.iceida.is/media/pdf/MBSP-MID-TERM-EVALUATION_FINAL.pdf.

OECD (2016), "Providers' use of results information for accountability, communication, direction and learning. Survey results, Iceland survey response", August 2016, OECD, Paris, www.oecd.org/dac/peer-reviews/Providers'_use_of_results_information_for_accountability_communication_direction_and_learning.pdf.

UNICEF (2014), "WASH for Children in Zambézia Province, Water supply, sanitation and hygiene in rural communities and schools (2014-2017)" http://www.iceida.is/iceida-projects/nr/4187

ORGANISATION FOR ECONOMIC CO-OPERATION AND DEVELOPMENT

The OECD is a unique forum where governments work together to address the economic, social and environmental challenges of globalisation. The OECD is also at the forefront of efforts to understand and to help governments respond to new developments and concerns, such as corporate governance, the information economy and the challenges of an ageing population. The Organisation provides a setting where governments can compare policy experiences, seek answers to common problems, identify good practice and work to co-ordinate domestic and international policies.

The OECD member countries are: Australia, Austria, Belgium, Canada, Chile, the Czech Republic, Denmark, Estonia, Finland, France, Germany, Greece, Hungary, Iceland, Ireland, Israel, Italy, Japan, Korea, Latvia, Luxembourg, Mexico, the Netherlands, New Zealand, Norway, Poland, Portugal, the Slovak Republic, Slovenia, Spain, Sweden, Switzerland, Turkey, the United Kingdom and the United States. The European Union takes part in the work of the OECD.

OECD Publishing disseminates widely the results of the Organisation's statistics gathering and research on economic, social and environmental issues, as well as the conventions, guidelines and standards agreed by its members.

DEVELOPMENT ASSISTANCE COMMITTEE

To achieve its aims, the OECD has set up a number of specialised committees. One of these is the Development Assistance Committee (DAC), whose mandate is to promote development co-operation and other policies so as to contribute to sustainable development – including pro-poor economic growth, poverty reduction and the improvement of living standards in developing countries – and to a future in which no country will depend on aid. To this end, the DAC has grouped the world's main donors, defining and monitoring global standards in key areas of development.

The members of the DAC are Australia, Austria, Belgium, Canada, the Czech Republic, Denmark, the European Union, Finland, France, Germany, Greece, Hungary, Iceland, Ireland, Italy, Japan, Korea, Luxembourg, the Netherlands, New Zealand, Norway, Poland, Portugal, the Slovak Republic, Slovenia, Spain, Sweden, Switzerland, the United Kingdom and the United States.

The DAC issues guidelines and reference documents in the DAC Guidelines and Reference Series to inform and assist members in the conduct of their development co-operation programmes.

www.ingramcontent.com/pod-product-compliance
Lightning Source LLC
Chambersburg PA
CBHW082344220526
45470CB00008B/2636